GLEN PARVA BARRACKS
BY DEREK SEATON

The building of Leicester Barracks (later to become known as Glen Parva Barracks) took place between 1876 and 1880. This was a direct result of Parliament passing the Military Forces Localisation Act 1872, which was part of a series of reforms to expand and modernise the British Army.

Initially, in 1874, the Government purchased 20 acres of the Grange estate in the tiny hamlet of Glen Parva, from Captain Philip Goodchild, for the building of the infantry barracks. Importantly, the southern boundary of the site adjoined the London & North Western Railway close to the area which shortly afterwards was developed into the village of South Wigston. The price paid for the land was £3,791. In 1875, the tender to erect the barracks for the sum of £66,500 (excluding extras) was submitted by Messrs Henry Everett & Son, building contractors of Colchester in Essex, and was accepted.

The barracks, which were designed to accommodate upwards of 500 troops, were ready for occupation in the spring of 1880 and were designated as the 27th Brigade Depot in the first instance.

In 1881 the old numbered Regiments of Foot were replaced by regiments with county titles, thus the 17th became The Leicestershire Regiment. The barracks were soon to become known as the Regimental Depot of The Leicestershire Regiment, the home of the county regiment.

Throughout the next thirty years, thousands of recruits passed through Glen Parva Barracks as The Leicestershire Regiment, affectionately known as 'The Tigers', served throughout the world. The 1st Battalion had fought with distinction in the Boer War, and by 1910 there were large numbers of veterans of the Siege of Ladysmith adding their individual and collective experience of war to the training of new recruits and soldiers coming through the ranks.

For some years the rival European powers had been competing over trade and the extension of their colonies. Military might and threatening alliances were growing and war clouds were on the horizon.

On Sunday, 2 April 1911, the last national census was taken before the world was plunged into war.

The census returns for Glen Parva Barracks are recorded as follows:

Officers	5
NCOs	47
Men	123
Total	175

Persons other than soldiers:

Wives	30
Children	64
Civilians	4
Visitors	4
Total	102

The number of people, both military and civilian, located at the depot by 1914 was comparatively low. Both the two regular battalions of The Leicestershire Regiment were stationed overseas. The 1st Battalion was in Fermoy, County Cork, Ireland, whereas the 2nd Battalion was undertaking a tour of duty in India and was stationed in Ranikhet. Thus the depot was then mainly occupied by permanent staff, instructors and recruits in small numbers. This was soon to change!

On 4 August 1914, Britain declared war on Germany as the major European countries aligned themselves into two main camps for the commencement of a titanic struggle that would forever be known as the First World War.

Within a week of the outbreak of the war some 1,100 reservists had been recalled, equipped and sent off from the depot, they marched away to the strains of Mr Charles Moore's Wigston Temperance Silver Prize Band.

Horses as well as men were urgently required and *The Leicester Mail*, reporting on Glen Parva Barracks on 10 August, stated: 'Fifty horses have been commandeered and were paraded on the Fairfield Green.' The intention

WIGSTON
IN THE FIRST WORLD WAR

WIGSTON
IN THE FIRST
WORLD WAR

Duncan Lucas, Derek Seaton,
Tricia Berry & Jean Dann

The
History
Press

*This book is dedicated to all service personnel who went from
Wigston to answer their country's call in the First World War
and never returned. We acknowledge their sacrifice with
gratitude and remember their loved ones left behind.*

Front cover image:
The firing party prepare to fire over the grave of Lieutenant-Colonel John
Edward Mosse. (Record Office for Leicestershire, Leicester and Rutland)

Back cover image:
'The Lion's Den'. British Tommies relaxing out of the line. (Duncan Lucas)

First published 2014

The History Press
The Mill, Brimscombe Port
Stroud, Gloucestershire, GL5 2QG
www.thehistorypress.co.uk

© Duncan Lucas, Derek Seaton, Tricia Berry & Jean Dann, 2014

The right of Duncan Lucas, Derek Seaton, Tricia Berry & Jean Dann to
be identified as the Authors of this work has been asserted in accordance
with the Copyright, Designs and Patents Act 1988.

British Library Cataloguing in Publication Data.
A catalogue record for this book is available from the British Library.

ISBN 978 0 7524 8835 6

Typesetting and origination by The History Press
Printed in Great Britain

CONTENTS

The Fountain, on the Bank, Wigston Magna. (Duncan Lucas)

INTRODUCTION

Wigston Magna and South Wigston, in the heart of tranquil Leicestershire, were transformed from their peaceful semi-rural existence in August 1914 as war swept across Europe. These adjoining villages, the homes of farming folk and framework knitters, suddenly witnessed their young men leaving in vast numbers to answer the call of King and Country.

Greater demands were placed upon those who remained, as the factories and farms responded to the needs of a wartime nation. Occupying a unique presence, within the boundaries of the Wigston Magna Urban District Council, was the Glen Parva Barracks, the Regimental Depot of The Leicestershire Regiment, where tens of thousands of recruits and conscripted men received their basic training to prepare them for war.

This is the story of the Wigstons, their fighting men, one of whom was awarded the Victoria Cross, and those who served on the home front. Each chapter seeks to portray a different aspect of what happened to one close-knit community during 'The war to end all wars'.

Derek Seaton, 2014

ACKNOWLEDGEMENTS

Our sincere thanks are extended to a number of people and organisations who so kindly contributed their time and knowledge, without which it would not have been possible to publish *Wigston in the First World War*.

We are extremely grateful to Richard Bettsworth, editor of *The Leicester Mercury*, for permission to use the photograph of Sergeant William Ewart Boulter VC and his parents (1916), and Adam Goodwin, archivist at the Record Office for Leicestershire, Leicester and Rutland for his interest in the project and his invaluable assistance. Also to other members of staff at the Record Office who dealt so efficiently with our many enquiries and our requests to have documents made available; permission to feature a number of photographs relating to Glen Parva Barracks and Wigston during the wartime years is also greatly appreciated.

We should also like to express our thanks to the following for their important contributions: Gerry Broughton, Janice Broughton, Peter Cousins, Mark Gamble, Colin Gore, Mick Rawle, Joan Rowbottom and Sue Shore.

We are extremely grateful to Daniel Tanner for his specialised assistance in assembling all of the illustrations, from various sources, in readiness for the publisher. His contribution was invaluable.

A special word of thanks must go to Matilda Richards of The History Press for her guidance, expertise and encouragement at all times.

Finally, we owe a huge debt of gratitude to Diane Batson for her work in word processing eight of the chapters, plus the framework of the book and for bringing the entire manuscript together as required by the publisher.

Duncan Lucas, Derek Seaton
Tricia Berry and Jean Dann

was to use local horses for transport duties but this in turn put an enormous strain upon local tradespeople and deliveries. One local firm of bakers, Messrs Black's Bread Co. Ltd, at No. 32 Charles Street, Leicester, was clearly irritated by the loss of its horses and inserted the following notice in the local press:

> HORSES COMMANDEERED BLACK'S BREAD CO. LIMITED beg to inform their customers that the Army having commandeered 10 of their best horses they will have great difficulty in delivering bread. They guarantee to call upon all their customers daily but must ask to be excused if they should be a little later than usual.

A week after the declaration of war, Field Marshall Earl Kitchener, the newly appointed Secretary of State for War, launched a massive recruitment campaign on 11 August. He called for 100,000 volunteers between the ages of 19 and 30 years and within three weeks his target had been well exceeded. This initial intake formed the First New Army (K1).

The command of the Regimental Depot, following the outbreak of war, was an all-important assignment. In this regard, The Leicestershire Regiment was fortunate in being able to call upon the services of a very experienced soldier and administrator in Lieutenant-Colonel John Edward Mosse, a retired Tiger.

Entrance to Glen Parva Barracks. (Duncan Lucas)

Lieutenant-Colonel John Mosse with his wife Catherine and their daughter Miss Sheila Mosse, together with two orderlies and the family dogs, outside of the Commandant's residence at the Regimental Depot. (Record Office for Leicestershire, Leicester and Rutland)

He had been commissioned into the regiment in 1879 and served for twenty-four years. Although on the retired list, he willingly offered his services and was duly appointed the commanding officer of Glen Parva Barracks in succession to Colonel George Burne.

Locally, the response to Earl Kitchener's call to arms was almost overwhelming. The sheer scale of new recruits put an enormous strain upon the administrative and training elements of the Regimental Depot as men enlisted in unprecedented numbers. Extra clerical staff had to be requisitioned for the recruiting at the barracks in order to cope with the additional workload, as upwards of 100 men a day were joining Kitchener's Army in the Leicester area.

The scene was vividly described in the *Leicester Advertiser* (4 September 1914): 'The number of recruits presenting themselves for all sections of the Army is increasing and as soon as they have been passed by the doctor and been sworn in they are drilled. The barracks square at Glen Parva has resounded to the incessant instructions of the drill sergeants.'

As a direct result of Earl Kitchener's call, four new battalions of Tigers were formed; they became the 6th, 7th, 8th and 9th (Service) Battalions of The Leicestershire Regiment, later to become the 110th Leicestershire Brigade.

Many men from the local factories, such as Messrs Two Steeples Ltd, hosiery manufacturers of Wigston Magna, joined up together to form the Pals' Battalions as they became known. The Managing Director, Mr Edward Lee, held a patriotic recruiting campaign at the factory and twenty-two men from the workforce answered the call of their boss. The lads were given a great send off by their fellow workers, many of whom accompanied them to Glen Parva Barracks as they joined the ranks of the 8th and 9th Battalions in September 1914.

Recruits for Kitchener's Army at Glen Parva Barracks in September 1914. (Duncan Lucas)

Fellow workers from Two Steeples Ltd pictured outside of Glen Parva Barracks on
3 September 1914, who gathered to wave off 'their boys'. (Duncan Lucas)

Despite all the best endeavours of the recruiting staff and instructors,
the sheer volume of new recruits turning up at the depot was beyond
their capabilities. Large numbers of men, at one stage up to 1,000 recruits,
had to be billeted with local residents in the streets of South Wigston.
An allowance of 2s a day was paid for each man in respect of food and
lodgings. South Wigston became a village 'invaded' by Kitchener's men.

As the newly formed Service Battalions of The Leicestershire Regiment
were prepared for war, the two regular battalions had arrived in France. The
1st Battalion took part in the retreat from Mons in September 1914 and was then
involved in the first battle of Ypres, which was concluded in November 1914.
Meanwhile, the 2nd Battalion reached the Western Front at the end of the year,
having arrived from India with the Garhwal Brigade of the Meerut Division of
the Indian Army Corps and also initially saw action at Ypres. Heavy casualties
were taken and replacements became a matter of urgency, putting a greater
demand upon the resources of Glen Parva Barracks to respond.

By the spring of 1915 recruitment had fallen dramatically, added to which
the 4th and 5th Territorial Battalions of the Regiment had arrived in France.
With four battalions now involved in or preparing for action on the Western
Front urgent replacements were required as the casualty lists mounted.

An important visitor to Glen Parva Barracks in April 1915 was Private
William Henry Buckingham VC, 2nd Battalion, The Leicestershire Regiment.
He had been awarded the Victoria Cross 'for conspicuous acts of bravery and
devotion to duty in rescuing and rendering first aid to the wounded whilst
exposed to heavy fire at Neuve Chapelle on 10 and 12 March 1915'. Following
medical treatment at South Manchester Hospital he returned to the depot

Two courageous members of the Recruiting Team based at the depot. Seated is
Lance-Corporal Thomas Newcombe DCM and holder of the Russian Cross of
St George. Standing is Private William H. Buckingham VC. (Record Office for
Leicestershire, Leicester and Rutland)

where he spent the next nine months as a member of the Regimental Recruiting Team. Under the command of Colour-Sergeant B. Payne, the small team was effective in recruiting men into the regiment. Meanwhile, the 110th Leicestershire Brigade was preparing to leave for France.

Private Buckingham eventually returned to France to join the 1st Battalion on the Western Front.

As the months went by and the casualties increased, Glen Parva Barracks' small hospital (two wards with fifteen beds in each) provided additional medical and recuperative care for a small number of soldiers. Often they would be taken, along with other wounded comrades, recovering in local hospitals, for tea and entertainment as guests of local organisations.

The Military Service Bill was presented before the House of Commons on 5 January 1916. The proposed legislation to introduce conscription was keenly debated and duly passed by Parliament with a huge majority. Conscription under the new Military Service Act commenced on 2 March, and was made general for unmarried men and widowers between the ages of 18 and 41 years. The Act was extended to include married men from 25 May onwards.

In the wake of the new legislation some men claimed exemption on a variety of grounds. They included a small number of conscientious objectors who refused to don a military uniform whereas others were prepared to serve with non-combatant units, for example as stretcher-bearers with the Royal Army Medical Corps.

Local Military Service Tribunals were established throughout the country, including Leicester, to consider applications for exemption. A large number of conscientious objectors were given non-combatant service and ordered to report to Glen Parva Barracks.

On 24 May 1916, twelve men appeared before the Police Court at the Town Hall in Leicester for 'failing to appear at the time and place at which they were required to do so' under the Act. With one exception they pleaded guilty and refused, on conscientious grounds, to serve either as combatants or non-combatants. Each of the accused was fined £2 and ordered to be handed over to the Military Authorities. Later in the day they were marched to Glen Parva Barracks under a military escort.

On 17 June 1916, whilst on duty at the barracks, Lieutenant-Colonel John Mosse, the Commandant of the Glen Parva Depot, collapsed in the orderly room and died the same day. His sudden and unexpected death from a stroke, at the age of 56, caused great distress throughout the depot where he was held in high regard by his fellow officers and was very popular with the NCOs and men.

The funeral of Lieutenant-Colonel John Mosse took place on Thursday 22 June. Large crowds of local residents lined the short route from the barracks to the Church of St Thomas the Apostle (the church was built in 1893 for the newly created Parish of Glen Parva with South Wigston and it became the Garrison Church for the depot). The colonel's coffin, draped by the Union Jack, was conveyed on a horse-drawn gun-carriage. The bearer party consisted of two sergeant-majors, two colour-sergeants and two quartermaster-sergeants from the barracks, with a firing party in attendance, detachments of troops and the depot band.

The funeral service was conducted by the vicar the Revd Trevor Spedding who also served as chaplain to the Regimental Depot. Following the service, the funeral procession proceeded to Welford Road Cemetery, Leicester, where Lieutenant-Colonel John Mosse was laid to rest.

Many tributes were paid to the late colonel in the local press, including one from the Mayor of Leicester, Alderman Jonathan North, who said of him: 'Lieutenant-Colonel John Mosse was a typical British soldier who held high ideals of duty and set an example which won him the confidence and esteem of the officers and men among whom he served.'

Further distress was felt at the depot when news was received of the death of Private William Henry Buckingham VC, who had been killed in action at the Battle of the Somme on 15 September 1916. He was, at the time, serving as personal orderly to Captain John Wilford Eric Mosse, Company Commander, 'A' Company of the 1st Battalion of The Leicestershire Regiment, and the son of the late Lieutenant-Colonel John Mosse.

The firing party prepare to fire three volleys as the coffin was lowered into the grave. (Record Office for Leicestershire, Leicester and Rutland)

The hectic hive of activity at Glen Parva Barracks showed no signs of lessening as the war progressed and, in February 1917, it was reported in the local press that District Courts Martial were held regularly at the depot. Often the senior officers served as President of the Court and other officers would be required to make up the court.

On 21 June 1917, the Bishop of Peterborough, the Right Revd Frank Theodore Woods, granted a licence for the erection of a brass plate in the Parish Church of St Thomas to honour the memory of the late Lieutenant-Colonel John Mosse. The plate, bearing the badge of The Leicestershire Regiment, read as follows:

> In memory of Lieutenant-Colonel John Edward Mosse, who died suddenly in the performance of his duty while in command of the Depot, The Leicestershire Regiment on the 17th June 1916 in his 56th Year. Erected as a tribute of affection and respect by the Officers, Warrant Officers, Non-Commissioned Officers and Men who served under him from the 4th August 1914.

The cost of the plate was met by contributions from all ranks who served with Lieutenant-Colonel John Mosse.

Sport always featured prominently in regimental depots and Glen Parva Barracks was no exception, as sporting activities continued throughout the wartime years. Soldiers and civilian recruiting staff held a Depot Sports Day on 1 September 1917. Activities were not confined entirely to sport as, in addition to the extremely competitive racing, it was reported in the *Leicester Advertiser* (8 August 1917): 'The general knowledge paper and the recruiting arithmetic competition caused much amusement and interest.' During the afternoon, selections were played by the Depot Band under the direction of Mr Dambman (Bandmaster). The prizes were presented by Mrs Drew, the wife of the Commanding Officer Lieutenant-Colonel Tom Maxwell Drew, who had taken over as Commandant. He had served with the 1st Battalion, The Leicestershire Regiment, was a veteran of the Boer War and had taken part in the Siege of Ladysmith.

The depot had a first-class football team and, during February 1918, they won every match in which they competed. Two significant results achieved were as follows: Depot *v.* Belper Road, Leicester, won 8–3, and Depot *v.* Leicester Balmoral, which they won 9–1.

The outstanding player was Lance-Corporal Henry Sarson, a centre forward who had scored almost 50 goals while playing for the depot team.

St Thomas the Apostle, South Wigston, the Garrison Church for Glen Parva Barracks.
(Derek Seaton)

On 9 February 1918 he was selected to play for Leicester Fosse in the club's away game against Sheffield United. (Leicester Fosse Football Club became Leicester City Football Club in 1919.) The Football League and Football Association Cup programmes had been suspended during the wartime years and the Fosse competed in the Midlands Section of the Football League. During the next five weeks, Lance-Corporal Sarson played for Leicester Fosse on three more occasions.

Entertainment for wounded soldiers at the depot continued to be a high priority. A report in the *Leicester Advertiser*, dated 4 May 1918, described a typical event:

> A grand concert was given in the dining room at the barracks, on 30 April, to entertain the wounded and convalescent soldiers. A varied programme of vocal and instrumental music was arranged by the well-known and popular bandmaster of South Wigston (Mr Charles Moore). Sergeant Payne presided and, at the close, thanked the artistes for their services.

Eventually the long, drawn-out and bloody First World War came to an end. When the news of the signing of the Armistice, on Monday, 11 November 1918, was received in Wigston Magna and South Wigston both villages were immediately decorated with streamers strung across the main roads.

On Thursday, 14 November a United Service of Praise and Thanksgiving was held at St Thomas' Church, at which there was a large congregation. The clergies of all the local denominations took part and the Military Depot was represented by the Commandant, Lieutenant-Colonel Tom Maxwell Drew.

The part played by Glen Parva Barracks, the Regimental Depot of The Leicestershire Regiment, was incalculable in terms of its contribution to the final victory. In preparing men for war and instilling in them pride in their local regiment, the barracks achieved all that Earl Kitchener desired when he drew up his plans for Britain's New Armies.

2

RECOLLECTIONS
BY DUNCAN LUCAS

The following was written by Frank Noble in 1979 shortly before his death.

In the following notes it is my intention to jot down a few facts and anecdotes in order to give an idea of what life in South Wigston was like in my earlier years and in the hope that these jottings will be of interest to some of the citizens of today and perhaps of tomorrow. I would not like to say that I shall get the correct chronological order after all these years but I trust that whoever may be interested will get the drift.

In advance I beg the indulgence of any of my readers for any grammatical or other errors. I left South Wigston Council School at the age of 13 years and English grammar was always my worst subject – 5 marks out of 10 was the best I could ever manage.

I was born in Glengate, South Wigston in the year 1907, but my mother always told me that we moved to live in Dunton Street when I was 3 years old. Nevertheless I can distinctly remember my grandfather who was a lamplighter, lifting me up in his arms to 'help' him light the street lamps in Glengate with the long pole which was always used for that purpose. As I remember it, this pole had a perforated metal contraption on the end inside which was a little flame (a paraffin wick? I don't know, I cannot remember). On the end of the metal piece was a hook. The hook to turn on the gas and the flame to ignite it.

I dimly remember my first day at school at the age of 3. To me it seemed a very large place and very dark. The seats rose in tiers like the 'gods' at the Leicester Palace. I don't remember much of my time in the infants' school except that the museum had a large ostrich egg in it. I remember that we celebrated Empire Day with the whole school parading in the playground waving little flags and singing songs of Empire.

Another day I remember celebrating as a boy was Oak Apple Day. Everyone was supposed to wear either an oak apple or an oak leaf. If they did not sport one of these they were open to attack with a bunch of stinging nettles. I believe it was to celebrate the occasion when King Charles hid from his enemies in an oak tree.

Another early memory is of the soldiers at the barracks in their scarlet tunics on sentry duty at the barrack gates just as they do today outside Buckingham Palace. The brave show of a church parade on a Sunday morning. The big drummer in his tiger's skin proudly swinging his drum sticks, the brass instruments glistening in the sun. Always a large contingent for St Thomas' Church and smaller ones for the chapels.

I had left the infant school and moved up into Standard One when the Great War started. One morning when on the way to school a battalion of the Leicesters marched along Blaby Road (four abreast in those days) on the way to entrain at the Spion Kop station. They stretched all the way from the top of the hill back along Blaby Road. We kids were entranced and cleared off to see all there was to see. Of course that made us late for school and we all had the cane. This was considered a matter of course and taken in our stride. No offence – justice had been done!

Later came the commandeering of horses. The greens on Dunton Street, Fairfield Street and Leopold Street were all full of them. The great shires, piebalds, blue bloods and the gypsy hacks, they were all there and the soldiers in charge camped among the horses. This was great fun for us lads. We sat round the camp fires and shared a mouthful out of the billy cans.

Another invasion of the village was by Kitchener's Army. These men were not in 'khaki' but in dark blue uniforms with a Glengarry hat, some were in 'civvies'. There must have been thousands of them. Every house had to take some in. I know there were four or five in our house. Even so there were not enough rooms for them all and some slept in the front gardens in Bassett Street.

Then came food shortages and there was no official rationing in those early days, just long queues at all the shops. As a boy I had instructions from my mother. If I saw a queue I was to find out what was being sold and run home to tell her. Times were getting tough. Writing paper disappeared from the school. We had to use slates and squeaky slate pencils. The younger male teachers disappeared too and lady teachers took their places much to the boys' disgust. They didn't know how to play 'rugger' and we didn't like having the cane from them either. A man, yes, but it wasn't dignified to have one from a lady.

I remember the Dunmore's biscuit firm had a supply of fruit pulp (not jam but near enough) which they sold to the public. The queue stretched three parts of

Kitchener's recruits with their NCOs, outside of No. 11 Bassett Street, South Wigston.
(Duncan Lucas)

the way down Canal Street. My mum didn't have to join that queue because
dad worked there and got his jar full while at work. How I hated the blackout
if I had to go out at night.

Then male teachers began to return, disabled but still fit enough to teach
us how to play rugger. Then came 11 November 1918, everywhere full
of excited rumours. The teachers didn't fetch us in from playtime and so
many of us cleared off to play Cowboys and Indians down the osier beds
on what is now the Magna Industrial Estate. There was a refuse tip down
there too, lovely places for exploring. Later that day curiosity led us back
to school to see what was happening in the real world of grown-ups and
we were promptly packed off home again by a stern-faced headmaster with
twinkling eyes and never a cane in sight. The Armistice had been signed.
Strange to say I remember little of the Victory Celebrations, only a lot of
flags and races in the nearby fields.

During my boyhood, South Wigston was a pleasant village to grow up in.
We had good teachers at school. Daddy Barwick as headmaster until he retired
and emigrated to Australia. He was replaced by Mr J.H. Butler. There was
also Billy Mew, 'Specs' Bryant, 'Hoppy' Reynolds and Ernie Powdrill; the two
latter being disabled ex-servicemen. I had the cane from them all many times.

I asked for it and got it. No hard feeling but a deep respect. Daddy Barwick's cane hurt least and Billy Mew's the most. In my day any boy who didn't have the cane was regarded as 'cissie'. What a change for the worse today. The cane when caught out never did a boy any harm, at least it teaches him to try not to be caught out next time.

3

HOME FRONT: 1914–1918
BY JEAN DANN

How did the people of Wigston deal with the enormity of a world war? Everyone had someone in their family away fighting or knew of a neighbour or friends involved with the military. The press were reporting the call up of volunteers by Lord Kitchener in terms of high resounding patriotism, and many responded.

The local churches and chapels were trying hard to come to terms with the conflict. They supported the troops abroad and comforted the bereaved at home.

There is a sense after reading their copious notes that they tried to 'get on with things' and endeavoured to maintain their various services and meetings. It had been widely felt that the war would be over by Christmas 1914. However, during late autumn the realisation set in that this was just the beginning.

Most of the churches and chapels produced a monthly magazine. The Revd Thomas Wright was the incumbent of All Saints' Church throughout the war years. Coming from the East End of London as a staunch Socialist often placed him at odds with local businessmen. In his address to his parishioners at the outbreak of war he referred to an article in a Unionist newspaper which questioned:

> Do we understand why we are fighting? Germany means to take our trade and colonies and to reduce us to a third rate power under the heel of the Kaiser and his generals. We are in a life or death struggle. We must know that victory will cost us dear but we must understand that defeat will mean ruin and shame as bitter as slavery.

In response, the Revd Wright commented: 'These are strong words and yet they seem to be none too strong in the face of what we already know. Is it too much to expect that our English mothers will urge and encourage their sons to serve with the colours as the mothers of all other countries are doing? England needs help and it must be given at once.'

Wigston Magna Urban District Council was going to play a large role in the war effort; however, on 24 August 1914 they were more concerned about excessive drinking in Wigston. They took the decision to close all public houses by eight o'clock. They were also unhappy that one of their horses had been requisitioned by the Government for the war effort and were unable to replace it until October.

The Reverend Thomas William Wright MA, Vicar of All Saints' Church, Wigston Magna. (Janice Broughton)

September saw South Wigston's barracks full to overflowing due to the huge response to Kitchener's appeal for volunteers. The Council's Finance Committee received a circular from the Local Government Board as to the difficulty of finding accommodation and suitable catering facilities for the large influx of new recruits and they were hoping that the Council could resolve the problem.

All Saints' Church. (Jean Dann)

By 25 September, Revd Wright commented to his parishioners that recruiting in the country had been brisk although the serious nature of the war had been unknown. 'Men do not want to be rushed into taking such a step unless they are convinced of its absolute importance. The horrors and cruelties practised upon innocent women, children and wounded men have stirred the hearts of those who hate such things to sacrifice everything to put this down.' He goes on to say: 'I believe that every strong man that holds back now when he could serve his King and Country must feel that people will be persecuted and killed because he holds back and in the end he will most likely be compelled to go.'

At the same time the *Wigston and District Free Churchman* magazine commented, '"Business as usual" this is the motto a newspaper correspondent suggested should be ours in this grave crisis. It is an eminently sane precept and in a wonderful way people have responded to it. At a time of unrivalled difficulty they have realised that they can best help by seeing to it that commercial and industrial life carry on as normal.'

Late in November the free churches held their annual meeting where one of the speakers addressed the assembly, saying: 'Victory will be ours, but we shudder to think of the price in blood and devastation. The ruin and barbarity displayed in Belgium by a ruthless enemy has made the whole world sick of war and has aroused the spirit of revenge. If ever we needed calmness and courage it is now.'

1915

Wigston wanted to honour its men who had volunteered for the armed services. Mr Brittan of South Wigston Conservative Club suggested that a Roll of Honour should be placed in the club to include members and members' sons serving in the military. They received news that Fred Norman had been wounded and was in a military hospital in Cardiff. All Saints' Church placed a Roll of Honour on the entrance door naming all men on active service and the church bell was rung each day at twelve o'clock to remind people to pray for peace.

Alcohol appeared to still be causing a problem. The military asked for all public houses to be closed even earlier. The Revd Wright stated that the King had given up alcohol and suggested that his parishioners do the same. He goes on to say, 'If the various political clubs and the leading men we have elected to represent us on the Urban District Council all decide to follow the King's example, would it not help many others to do the same?'

The Wigston Primitive Methodists were concerned that the war was still raging and they had received sad news that Arthur Boothaway of Central Avenue had been killed on 2 January; he had been one of their Sunday School scholars, and his death was a severe blow to the church and his family.

The war was also beginning to tell in people's pockets and the Council was becoming increasingly concerned about the ever-rising cost of living. They had decided not to take on new coal contracts and to extinguish gas street lamps at nine o'clock each evening with the exception of those close to the railway station. By April the decision was taken to turn lamps off altogether until August and not to light them until Leicester lit theirs. One of the ways soldiers were able to help their families back home was with a Separation Allowance. The amounts were small and soldiers had to contribute from their army pay. The Government increased the rates slightly by 1 March.

One of the few ways Wigston people were able to contact their loved ones was by post. So when the postmaster in Leicester decided to curtail the service by closing the post office every Thursday afternoon and during the evening it must have been a blow for people who used the service regularly.

The Revd Wright received a letter on 24 March from his brother serving in France, which he reproduced in the church magazine. It gave his parishioners a glimpse of the conditions the men were in.

We had our first experience of shell fire last night. We are sleeping in a loft over cowsheds, our haversacks as pillows. I was woken up last night by a rat tugging at my pillow to get at some biscuits. We are now watching our guns shell a German flying machine. I hope they will get it.

By April 1915 Britain had 130,000 casualties, and Revd Wright appealed for more men to join up: 'We need more men if this hideous tragedy is to end. I have been criticised for not encouraging "pleasure as usual" but I cannot. As our own dear ones get out in the trenches many will think as I do.'

On 15 June an appeal to the nation for 'thrift' was introduced by Prime Minister Herbert Asquith and War Loans were launched. Later in the year people could purchase strips of vouchers from 5s upwards. The intention was that the country could pay for the war itself rather than rely on borrowing. There was also a push to reduce imports of tea, tobacco, wine, sugar and petrol.

As August approached, Wigston appeared to still be reeling with the extent of the war. South Wigston Wesleyan Church held a memorial service where the Roll of Honour was read aloud. When it came to the names of Sergeant Henry Ruckledge and Private Gordon Sutton, both of The Leicestershire Regiment,

The Post Office and Drapery Shop (left), No. 36 Bell Street, Wigston Magna, owned by
Edwin George Shipp. (Duncan Lucas)

the haunting sound of the last post rang out from the cornets of Wigston
Temperance Silver Prize Band.

Also that month, the Council had received a circular from the Local
Government Board informing them that: 'All statutory elections of the Urban
District Council which would occur prior to 1 July 1916 are postponed for
a year.' It was probably felt that with so many men at the front, elections would
not provide a fair decision. It is to be remembered that women could not vote.

Wigston hosiery factories were having something of a boom time
producing goods for the war effort. In September, Revd Wright wrote a
scathing report to his parishioners deploring that someone was hoping that
the war would 'last a lifetime' because profits were so good. 'To know that the
man wants the war to last for the sake of gains to himself is already inhaling
the poison gas of hell.' Unfortunately he doesn't tell us who the person was.
Later, the Government brought in an Excessive Profits tax to reduce gains,
plus a series of measures that made wool harder to obtain.

Also that month the All Saints' church magazine printed a letter from the front:

The weather is not the best. We were nearly washed out of our dugout,
in fact some of our chaps had to take shelter in a sap at about 3 a.m.
The water rose so high outside that it ran into the sap and again sopped
them. I am sitting in clothes wet to the skin and watching my tunic, which
I have taken off, dripping into a tin. I may say that we are all sopped to the
skin but still merry.

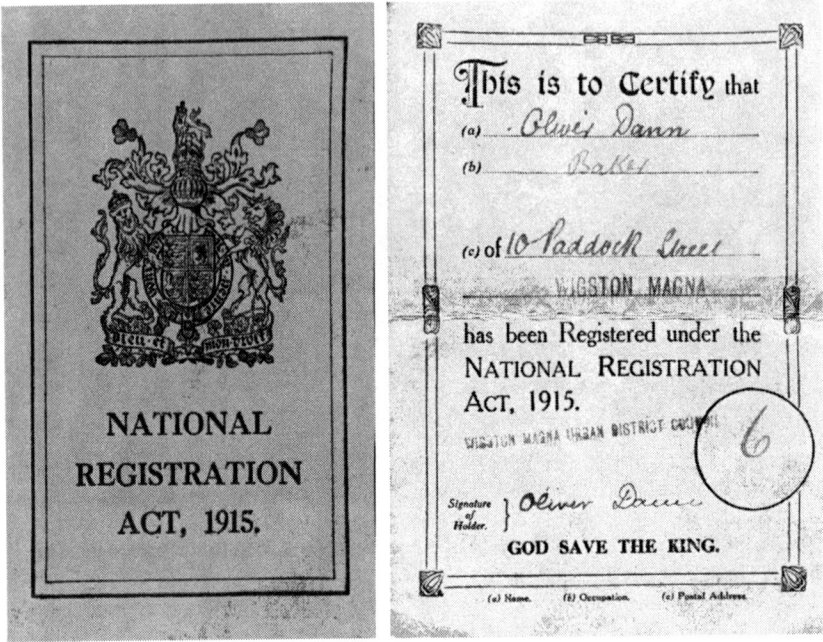

Oliver Dann's National Registration Card. (Jean Dann)

The National Registration Act of 1915 had come into force on 15 July, which provided a register of all persons between the ages of 15 and 65. Recruitment had slowed down and more men were needed and this Act provided names and employment of the population. The Council undertook the enumerating work which was completed by September.

By November, the Council had been instructed to set up a Military Service Tribunal. The aim of the tribunal was to decide questions for the Recruiting Authorities as to whether men should be spared from their current occupations and 'exempt' from the army. The Council had misgivings as to whether they should be the responsible body to make these decisions. However, they had no choice and a tribunal was formed.

1916

The implementation of the Military Service Act 1916, which introduced conscription, had a profound effect on men below the age of 41 years. There were very few automatic exemptions, however, men could apply to the Council's newly formed Military Service Tribunal for exemption status. The tribunal received a request from Mr Chapman whom it was thought necessary should stay in his post as engineer at Wigston Fields Pumping Station. His request had been accepted but as the Act went through its further stages in 1918 he had still been called to the colours. Clergy were automatically exempt.

Men were called up according to 'class' or age. It began with unmarried men, but later older married men were being called up. For example, my grandfather, Oliver Dann, was called to the colours by May 1916. He was with the 8th (Service) Battalion, The Leicestershire Regiment. By early 1918 he was discharged due to ill health and awarded the Silver War Badge. My grandmother said he came home a broken man. For a long time afterwards he had severe nightmares but like many returning soldiers he would never speak about his experiences at the Front.

Wigston manufacturers were finding it increasingly difficult to find suitable men to employ. They began by employing men from the exemption list, which included men discharged from the army, those who had a disability, or those too old for service, those rejected for enlistment for various reasons. But the exemptions would change within the year.

By February, lighting restrictions for properties were in place. All Saints had moved their evening services into the afternoons. The Council distributed leaflets advising people of the new regulations and precautions they should take if there was an air raid. In that eventuality, hooters on Messrs Dunmore & Sons, a biscuit factory in South Wigston, and Two Steeples hosiery factory would be sounded.

Oliver Dann, his wife, Eliza, and son, Ernest. (Jean Dann)

W4203—8414 200,000   7/16 HWV(M1897)   H16/1308
11572—R2757 200,000   12/16

No. **333653**

WAR BADGE awarded to _____ *O. Dann.*
                                              (Name)

late No. _45520_ **LEICESTERSHIRE REGT**
                          (Regimental Number and Unit)

for "Services Rendered" in H.M.'s Military Forces since 4th August, 1914.

Station _LICHFIELD._

Date _25·2·18_

Oliver Dann's Silver War Badge. (Jean Dann)

Institutions and factories took the precaution of insuring against aircraft damage caused by airships and bomber raids, including All Saints' Church, the Congregational Church in Long Street, Wigston Hosiers in Paddock Street and Henry Bates Hosiery Company in South Wigston amongst others. Individual householders could also purchase insurance from the post office from 6*d*.

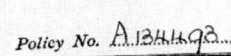
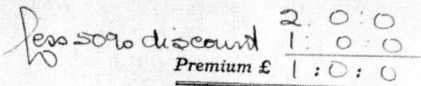

Policy No. A13414.92..... *less 50% discount* 2. 0 : 0
                                                1 : 0 : 0
                            Premium £ 1 : 0 : 0

This Policy is issued
through the agency
of the
ALLIANCE ASSURANCE
COMPANY, LIMITED.
Head Office:
Bartholomew Lane,
London, E.C.

GOVERNMENT
AIRCRAFT INSURANCE.

THIS POLICY OF INSURANCE made the *tenth* day
of *March* 1914 , WITNESSETH *that* in consideration
of *the Vicar & Churchwardens of Wigston Magna*

(hereinafter called the Insured) paying to HIS MAJESTY'S GOVERNMENT
(hereinafter called the Government) the premium above mentioned, for insuring,
as hereinafter mentioned, the following property, viz.:—

All Saints' Church fire-insurance document. (Janice Broughton)

By July, Wigston had lost about twenty men and a Memorial Service
was held at All Saints' Church where the last post was sounded. The church
provided a 'war corner' where people could remember and pray for all serving
men. Private Ernest Seaton of the 6th (Service) Battalion, The Leicestershire
Regiment, received a head wound from which he later died. He was the
first Wigston soldier to be returned to the village for burial from a military
hospital in England.

Also that month, the Council were notified by the National War
Savings Committee to form a war saving association in Wigston. A public
open-air meeting was held on Friday, 4 August at the Orchard Estate.
Another two meetings were set up at Goal Close and South Wigston Girls'
School. The object was to encourage thrift and economy during the war.
Mr Albert Edward Hill, JP was chairman whilst Mr Coley from All Saints'
Church was secretary. Contributions were collected from individuals
and companies.

In November another Memorial Service was held at All Saints' Church.
William Heard, Frederick Looms, Thomas Brindley, Joseph Brewin and Oliver
Hipwell were the latest men to lose their lives. The number of names on the
War Shrine had risen to eighty-one. Another man to fall was the foreman
of the local fire brigade, George Melville Proctor, who had been killed in
Mesopotamia, leaving the fire brigade even more severely undermanned. It
had already been called out seven times for air raids.

1917

The year of 1917 began with more concerns over the amount of alcohol being consumed. Nationally the food controller had placed a 30 per cent restriction on the manufacture of beer which, according to Revd Wright, released an extra 80 million tons of sugar. He hoped that the Government would cease making alcohol altogether so that shipping could bring more important food into the country. Overall, food supply was becoming difficult. The Board of Agriculture ordered local councils to seize unoccupied land, allowing the Council to cultivate the land themselves or arrange for others to do it on their behalf. Notice had been given to two lots of trustees. Firstly, the trustees of the late J.C. Clarke for land on the Orchards, and secondly the trustees of the late Orson Wright for land in South Wigston.

To further increase food supply, Council allotment holders could apply to purchase seed potatoes at cost price, plus restrictions were lifted on the distance pigs could be kept from dwellings. Leaflets were distributed to ask people to reduce food consumption as long as there was no detriment to health or efficiency. The Government also wanted to increase the importance of utilising waste food, waste paper and cardboard and whatever else was practicable to prevent waste.

Up to 5 tons 6 cwt of potatoes were distributed to allotment holders and the Council provided a potato sprayer. With the introduction of the Local Authorities Food Control Order came the directive that food must be protected. The Council decided they would pay 1s per dozen for rats' tails, 3d per dozen for the heads of fully fledged house sparrows, 2d per dozen for the heads of unfledged house sparrows and 1d a dozen for house sparrow eggs. People were encouraged to preserve fruit and vegetables and the Council supervised the distribution of sugar for jam making.

The Council's Food Control Committee was spending most of its time making orders for rationing food. Food had been short but now it was critical. Sugar certificates were issued to retailers and manufacturers; butchers were sent details on what they should be charging for meat; wholesale and retail potato certificates were distributed and sugar cards sent out, and certificates for bacon, lard and butter were produced.

One of the most unusual war requests came from the National Salvage Council when they asked people to collect fruit stones and nutshells.

With the summer came 'Baby Week'. A parade of prams left Wigston Hall and processed to Mrs Broughton's home in Aylestone Lane where a 'Mother Craft Exhibition' was underway. The Council put in motion a conference of local nursing associations for child and maternity welfare. Later in the year a three-day exhibition was held in the Co-operative Hall. It was entitled the 'Baby Club' and featured a travelling exhibition, including lectures on child life, models of cots, clothes, food and bottles. Babies were now important and valued. The Revd Wright commented: 'What a different place England will become if we really take care of our babies.'

Wigston had just recovered from a measles epidemic. Schools had been closed and the military authorities had placed South Wigston 'out of bounds' for soldiers from the barracks. A total of 141 cases had been reported. The year ended with another epidemic, this time whooping cough, which had broken out at Bell Street Infants' School. The school was closed until 20 February 1918.

The Army was short of men: those who had previously left the service due to health problems or who had been wounded were re-examined and where possible re-enlisted. The loss of men placed further pressure on Wigston's manufacturers.

Although the clergy were exempt from serving in the forces, the Government had introduced an Enrolment of Volunteers scheme. Mr Coley from All Saints' Church offered himself for war work in February 1917. The Revd Wright had also offered his services, but had to continue ministering in Wigston. The chapels also reported that some of their ministers in the union had volunteered. On Sunday, 23 September 1917 All Saints' Church held a Requiem Eucharist and dedicated the War Shrine; many family members and friends of the brave soldiers were present. Mr Charles Hurst was the designer of the War Shrine and Mr J.W. Barnes completed the lettering. Many contributions had been received from friends and relatives of the soldiers, together with money from teachers and children of the church school. The shrine would eventually hold the names of 126 men.

1918

This year began with a surprise cut in the cost of potatoes; 6cwt of margarine was ready for distribution amongst retailers in readiness for rationing, and children were given priority when milk regulations came in on 14 January. 7,500 people in Wigston were registered for meat rationing cards. Children between the ages of 6 and 10 had been given 'full' ration cards. Bakers were instructed to use potatoes with their flour. To reinforce the rules on food, Wigston appointed a prosecutor to deal with breaches of regulations.

Both · British · Bre(a)d

Before the War both these
                  two things
Were badly underrated,
But now they're valued properly
And both appreciated.

'Both British Bre(a)d' postcard. (Jean Dann)

ALL SAINTS' CHURCH,
WIGSTON MAGNA.

SUNDAY, SEPTEMBER 23rd, 1917,
AT 11-0 A.M.

REQUIEM EUCHARIST,

Offered on behalf of the
Wigston Men and Lads
———— who have ————
FALLEN in the WAR,

In the presence of the Right Reverend Father in God, the

LORD BISHOP OF LEICESTER

Who will Preach at the Service,
and afterwards

Dedicate the War Shrine.

———

By kind permission of Lieut. Colonel Drew, commanding Depot Leicestershire Regiment, a party of N.C.O. and Soldiers will attend from Glen Parva Barracks, under the command of Captain H. A. M. Worsley.

Pamphlet for the dedication of the War Shrine at All Saints' Church, 1917. (Janice Broughton)

Wigston Gas Works had 10 tons of coke in stock and were encouraging people to use it. The pit price of coal had increased by *2s 6d* per ton and by 1½*d* per hundredweight and would rise again. The Council were seeking advice on the future legislation for the rationing of household coal and later on Mr Oliver Hurst of Station Road was appointed Fuel Overseer at £105 per year.

In June the Council were still issuing food permits, this time to manufacturers and dealers and included bread, flour, bacon, tea and butter: 7,200 butter and margarine cards were issued to the population. By July the Food Committee had decided to increase the amount of brawn, tripe, chitterlings, horse flesh, pigs feet and cow heels people could get with their ration cards. The rationing of meat, fats and sugar was to commence on 13 July.

By 30 July it was reported that Wigston's population was estimated at 7,849, with 112 births and 110 deaths in the last year. Infant mortality was 62 per 1,000, compared to 97 in the rest of England and Wales. There were seventeen reported cases of TB and 195 cases of measles.

Between 30 September 1915 and June 1918 a total of 1,012 men had enlisted, and 160 men from Wigston and South Wigston had lost their lives – 1,718 men and 2,915 women were on the National Register. However, even worse was to come in October, when the Revd Wright was spending much of his time with the sick: a serious influenza pandemic had hit the community.

4

BELGIAN REFUGEES
BY TRICIA BERRY

The Kaiser's initial war strategy, the Schlieffen Plan, was to avoid a prolonged conflict on two fronts by a quick defeat of France, before the enemy in the East, Russia, had time to mobilize. To this end, he tried to broker a deal with Belgium for his army and equipment to have uninterrupted passage through their country. When this request was refused the revenge was terrible. *The Leicester Daily Mercury* of 4 August 1914 reported via the Press Association: 'The violation of Belgian neutrality by Germany is now an accomplished fact. The Government has received official information from the Belgian Government that the German forces have crossed into Belgian soil. The German army is advancing on to France.' Six days later the paper quoted the words of Father Caus of St Peter's Catholic Church, King Richard's Road, Leicester, who was a Belgian national: 'Invaded without reason or warning dear little Belgium which he [the Kaiser] had expected to win over by bribery and make of it a convenience to invade France … and eventually England.'

By 29 August the paper was reporting:

The famous Flemish town of Louvain is destroyed … The Germans shot some of their own … to cover their mistake they said it was the Belgians … The German commander without listening to any protest ordered the town to be destroyed … the inhabitants ordered to leave their dwellings, some of the men were made prisoners, the woman and children put on trains … destination unknown. Soldiers furnished with bombs set fire to the town … some VIP's were shot. The 85,000 inhabitants, the intellectual metropolis of the Low Countries since the 15th Century, is now no more than a heap of ashes … once a town of Flemish weavers.

Belgian refugees with Father Caus. (Record Office for Leicestershire, Leicester and Rutland)

The response was rapid: Britain sent a £10 million loan to Belgium, and France did the same. A National Belgian Relief Fund was established in Britain to appeal for donations of money and clothing etc.

By the beginning of September, refugees fleeing the chaos started to arrive in Britain and also the Netherlands and France. They arrived here at the invitation of the Government, which had announced a programme of State hospitality to the Belgian refugees. The Local Government Board, under its president Herbert Louis Samuel, and the War Refugee Committee were responsible for making the necessary arrangements. Most were initially taken to large holding buildings around London and the ports of entry. Here the Salvation Army organised food and clothing, and each person was registered and identity documents issued. They were then moved throughout the country into the care of local town and county War Refugee Committees. These committees were all very busy appealing for help, for which there was a generous response. Offers of accommodation, rent free or at a reduced rate, fuel, gifts of furniture, of food and clothes and services of all kinds came in, as well as money to the National Belgian Relief Fund which would now be used to support Belgians in Britain, as well as for distribution in their own country.

Comic postcards on topical subjects were popular in the early years of the twentieth century; those such as this one by the artist Donald McGill being particularly well known. (Tricia Berry)

Sydney Ansell Gimson was a Leicester Councillor and became Chairman of the Leicester Borough Refugee Committee. By the end of January 1915 there were 500 Belgians in the town, and they had formed a group, the Cercle Belge de Leicester. Including gifts in kind, the loan of houses, entertainment of guests in private houses etc., not less than £30,000 in value was given by Leicester people for the relief of the Belgians. (Sydney Gimson's later family home was to be Stoneywell in Ulverscroft, which has recently been acquired by the National Trust. It was designed for him by his brother Ernest Gimson, the Arts and Crafts architect and furniture maker. Both Sydney and Ernest were sons of the engineer and iron founder, Josiah Gimson.) In recognition of his work in raising the funds and helping the Belgian people in Leicester with the many problems their situation caused, he was decorated by the King of the Belgians.

William Allport Brockington MA was Director of Education for Leicestershire County Council and became Secretary of the Leicester County Refugee Committee. By 30 September 1914 he had received offers of accommodation for 800 Belgian men, women and children who were duly sent by the War Refugees Committee in London, and the Government representative in Folkestone. By January 1915 there were 1,000 in the county, and during the war a total of 2,000 were received and not less than £12,000 in value was subscribed for them. William Brockington was also decorated by the King of the Belgians. Later in his career he was knighted for his services to education, and Brockington College, Enderby, was named after him.

Most of the county Belgians were housed in Coalville, Loughborough, Hinckley, Melton Mowbray and Market Harborough, but the villages also took their share. *The Leicester Daily Post* of 17 September 1914 stated that: 'Waterloo House on the corner of Hastings Street and New Walk [Leicester] was being used as a clearing house … so far families comprising 40 people including 22 children have arrived in Leicester under the auspices of the Catholic League. Most are going to houses on the estate of Normanton Hall.'

In Wigston a local Belgian Refugee Committee was formed, which met in a room at the Council School, in Long Street. (This building now houses the Leicestershire, Leicester and Rutland Record Office.) The Revd Thomas William Wright, in the September issue of the *Parish Magazine*, reported: 'The Belgian Refugee Fund has received so far nearly £20 from the village, £10 from the concert in the Co-operative Hall and £9.10s. in answer to my appeal last month.' And in the October issue: 'We have received £22 from Wigston and we have in mind a scheme by which we as a village hope to offer shelter and hospitality to a number of Belgians. A cottage has been taken in the village, and the Girl Guides and the Boy Scouts are proposing to do their utmost to maintain a small family by denying themselves in various ways and enlisting the help of other children in the village. Also the village … is hoping to secure Wigston Grange … beds, bedding, furniture, kitchen utensils etc., will be needed … if we can get it.'

The Grange in Leicester Road, Wigston, is now occupied by the Institution of Occupational Safety & Health. It had been built in around 1820 by the Burgess family, and was a comfortable gentleman's residence, with 94 ½ acres of land. In 1876, following the death of Thomas Burgess, it was sold to three brothers, Alfred, Josiah and Henry Peters Tyler. They were a leading boot and shoe manufacturers and retailers with a chain of shops throughout the country. After the purchase, the owners, who all lived in Leicester, employed staff to run the farm and Albert Edward Tyler (probably a relative) lived in the house. By 1885 Albert had moved away and the brothers, having decided to give up farming, sold the livestock and produce and let out the house and land separately. The land remained in agricultural use for sometime but was eventually sold for building the Grange estate. Back in 1914, the Tyler family still owned the house which included the gardens, orchards and two fields, but was then unoccupied. Alfred and Henry Peters Tyler had died and it was owned by Josiah Tyler and a number of his nephews. No less than eight members of the Tyler family had to be asked for their permission to allow Belgian Refugees to be housed in their property.

The appeal for the Wigston Belgian Relief Fund (for local use) was very successful with many generous contributions from individuals and a number of factory collections. The first subscribers list up to 16 November 1914 totalled £126 18s 6d. It was published in the *Parish Magazine* and also in the *Wigston and District Free Churchman* by the Financial Secretary, John Alfred Broughton.

The Grange (*c.* 1915) (Tricia Berry)

Broughton was a partner in J.D. Broughton & Sons Hosiery Manufacturers, of Bell Street. He lived at Beech House, Aylestone Lane, which has now been demolished and replaced by the residential home, Beech Court.

By the following month a further £42 4s 3d had been donated to the fund. The Vicar announced that The Grange had been secured and many people had donated furniture, which Eli Bailey of Bushloe End, the local carter and farmer, had offered to transport. Albert George Shipp, a coal merchant who lived at Rowan House, No. 86 Bull Head Street, had promised a regular free supply of coal for The Grange during the residence of the refugees. Local boys from the church and council schools had helped with the carting, and the children of both schools and their parents had been sending meat, flour, butter, milk etc. week by week to help fill the stores. Albert Edward Hill, the owner of A.E. Hill Hosiery Manufacturers, of No. 25 Frederick Street, had offered the use of a cottage in North Street rent free, and Francis Hickling Freckingham of No. 22 Long Street, a butcher and grazier, had similarly offered a rent-free cottage in Mowsley End.

Wigston Belgian Relief Fund.

ₜₕE have much pleasure in publishing the first list of subscriptions up to and including Nov. 16th to the Local Belgian Relief Fund. The Committee has been able through the generosity of the inhabitants of Wigston to furnish The Grange and three cottages for the reception of the Refugees. To support these "strangers within our gates" requires considerable outlay, and the Hon. Financial Secretary (Mr. J. A. Broughton, Beech House) will be glad to receive new subscriptions in addition to those already promised.

	£	s.	d.
Mrs. Owston	15	0	0
Mr. H. T. Hincks and family	13	13	0
Mr. J. D. Broughton	10	10	0
Mr. Morley	10	0	0
Mr. E. Broughton	5	0	0
Mr. J. A. Broughton	5	0	0
Mr. B. Broughton	2	2	0
Mr. W. H. Sharp	2	2	0
Mr. Norman Sharp	1	0	0
Miss Elsie Sharp	0	10	6
Mr. and Mrs. J. T. Cooper	2	2	0
Mrs. Abbott	1	0	0
Miss Abbott	0	10	0
Mr. A. Abbott	0	10	0
Mr. Thomas Goodin	1	1	0
Mrs. Goodin	1	1	0
Miss Goodin	0	10	6
Mr. E. Goodin	0	10	6
Mr. and Mrs. Harrold	0	10	0
Mrs. Freckingham	0	5	6
Mrs. W. S. Cox	0	5	0
Teachers of C. of E. Infant School	0	5	0
Mr. George Wise	0	1	0
Mr. F. Simpson	0	5	0
Collection—All Saints' Church (1-11-14)	10	16	2
Mr. W. J. R. Pochin	7	7	0
Miss Boulter	1	0	0
Mr. J. H. Holmes (promise £3) 1st payment	0	10	0
Mr. J. Y. Hassall	1	0	0
Mrs. Brook	1	0	0
The Misses Hardy	0	5	0

	£	s.	d.
Mrs. Boulter	0	1	0
Mr. Huckle	0	5	0
Mrs. Taylor	0	5	0
Members of Wigston Conservative Club	5	0	0
Mr. T. Judd	1	1	0
Mr. Joseph Hassall	0	10	0
Mr. Jelly (promise of £2 10s.) 1st payment	0	10	0
Mr. W. F. Hurst	0	5	0
Mr. E. Clarke (Kilby Bridge)	0	5	0
Mr. W. H. Draper	0	2	6
Mrs. Harrison (Leicester Road)	0	5	6
Per Garrison Lecture	7	5	3
Collection at Public Meeting	5	15	0
Mrs. J. G. Phillips (per sale of John Oxenham's hymn)	0	15	0
Messrs. J. Watson & Sons, Leeds (Matchless Cleanser)	3	3	0
Half 10th Weekly Collection, Employees, J. D. Broughton & Sons	0	19	6
Half 10th Weekly Collection, Employees A. E. Hill	0	8	9
Half 3rd Monthly Collection, Employees Two Steeples Ltd.	1	2	0
Half 2nd Monthly Collection, Employees Cook & Hurst Ltd.	0	7	2
Half 4th Collection, Wigston Sanitary Steam Laundry	0	10	0
Mr. and Mrs. W. Wright	2	2	0
Balance from Red Cross Sewing Meeting	0	8	8
	£126	18	6

First list of subscribers to the Wigston Belgian Relief Fund. (*Wigston and District Free Churchman*, December 1914)

John Alfred Broughton, Honorary Financial Secretary of the Wigston Belgian Relief Fund, is on the right. The other two gentlemen (Bertram, left, and Ernest, centre) are his brothers and fellow directors at J.D. Broughton & Sons, hosiery manufacturers, Bell Street. (Tricia Berry)

Cottages in Mowsley End. (Tricia Berry)

The contributions continued each month with donors now including such diverse groups as schoolteachers, men's and women's adult schools, Amateur Dramatic Society, Wigston Band, All Saints' and St Wolstan's Churches, both congregation and choir, the Co-operative Education Committee, All Saints' Football Club, the Conservative Club, Parish and Congregational Mothers' Meetings, Wigston Gas Company, Sanitary Steam Laundry and the Midland Railway Carriage and Wagon Department. By 18 February 1915 the total collected had reached £275 0s 3d and it is pleasing to note that the male refugees were themselves contributing to the fund, showing that some at least had managed to obtain work. By 18 October 1915 the total collected had reached £395 17s 4d.

Wigston Magna Committee Local Belgian Relief Fund.

FOURTH LIST.

	£	s.	d.
Amount previously acknowledged ...	217	7	0
Miss Pochin	2	2	0
Mr. and Mrs. J. A. Harris	2	2	0
Mr. Jelley—3rd and 4th donations (10/- each)	1	0	0
Mrs. J. D. Broughton—4th donation ...	0	10	0
Mr. J. H. Holmes—4th donation ...	0	10	0
The Girl Guides—per Miss Barnley ...	1	2	2
Eva Rawlings and Stella Gamble—by making and selling paper flowers ...	0	8	0
Mrs. Cheney	0	5	0
Mr. W. Holmes—2nd donation ...	0	4	0
„ **W. Brewin**—2nd donation ...	0	2	0
„ **C. Boothaway**—2nd donation ...	0	4	0
„ **A. Boothaway**—2nd donation ...	0	1	0
Part Proceeds All Saints' Nativity Play—per Rev. T. W. Wright	2	0	0
Parish Church Mothers' Meeting—per Rev. T. W. Wright	1	10	0
Anonymous—per Rev. T. W. Wright ...	0	1	6
Men's and Women's Adult School—per Mrs. Johnson—3rd donation	1	0	6
Collected in Box at Conservative Club ...	0	3	6
Discounts from Tradesmen's Accounts ...	0	11	0
A friend—per Mr. W. H. Sharp ...	0	10	10
Dividend on purchases at Co-operative Society—per Mr. W. H. Sharp ...	0	18	0
Contribution towards maintenance by Male Refugees	2	6	0
The Mothers' Meeting—Congregational Church—per Mrs. J. A. Broughton ...	0	12	0
Interest from London City and Midland Bank	0	3	3

The whole of the Collections now made at the Factories and Schools of Wigston are devoted to the Local Belgian Relief Fund, and are as below :—

	£	s.	d.
Employees Messrs. J. D. Broughton & Sons			
20th collection ...	1	9	5½
21st collection ...	1	10	3
22nd collection ...	1	10	5
23rd collection ...	1	9	8
24th collection ...	1	9	7
Employees Mr. A. E. Hill—			
21st and 22nd collections ...	1	0	8
23rd and 24th collections ...	1	4	2
Employees Co-operative Society—			
5th collection ...	1	14	11
6th collection ...	1	14	2
Employees Mr. Chas Lewin—			
15th collection ...	0	18	6
16th collection ...	0	17	10
Employees Mr. W. H. Sharp—			
16th collection ...	0	10	6
17th collection ...	0	13	2
Employees Wigston Hosiers Ltd.—			
3rd collection ...	0	18	1½
Employees Messrs. W. Holmes & Son—			
5th collection ...	0	12	8
The Teaching Staffs Wigston Council and National Schools—6th collection ...	2	4	0
Employees Wigston Sanitary Steam Laundry ... ... 8th collection ...	1	0	0
Employees Messrs. Two Steeples Ltd—			
6th collection ...	1	9	6
Employees Messrs. Cook & Hurst Ltd.—			
5th collection ...	0	14	2
Employees Wigston Gas Company ...	1	0	0
Employees Midland Rly. Loco Dept.—			
9th collection ...	4	2	9
Employees South Wigston Shoe Co.—			
1st donation ...	1	2	0
Employees Messrs. Orson Wright & Son—			
1st donation ...	10	0	0
Total received to 18th Feb. 1915 ...	**£275**	**0**	**3**

In addition to the Collection taken and acknowledged above at Messrs. Two Steeples Ltd., 37 of their girls (led by Miss Tebbutt) are giving 3½ lbs. Butter weekly.

Further contributions will be gladly received by

J. A. BROUGHTON,

Hon. Fin. Sec., Beech House.

———

The last three items in the **February** Parish Magazine were added through misunderstanding ; they belong to March account, and have therefore been acknowledged again to save any discrepancy in accounts published in the two Magazines.—J.A.B.

Fourth list of subscribers to the Wigston Belgian Relief Fund. (*Wigston and District Free Churchman,* March 1915)

South Wigston and Glen Parva Belgian Relief Fund Balance Sheet
(FIRST QUARTER).

RECEIPTS.	£	s.	d.	EXPENDITURE.	£	s.	d.
By various small donations previous to organised collections	2	6	1½	To Expenses entailed in opening 3 houses	3	3	9½
Proceeds of Concert	20	0	8¼	Mr. Freeman's furniture account ...	7	3	7
Electrical Exhibition (per Mr. McKechnie)	2	0	2¾	Upkeep of Blaby Road house ...	16	6	4
DONATIONS :—				,, Healey Street house ...	14	0	4
Mrs. Gonder (per Mr. Beeston) ...	0	10	0	,, Irlam Street house ...	2	16	9
Mrs. Marsden (per Mr. J.W. Black, C.C.)	1	0	0	Rent of Blaby Road house ...	4	1	3
Sir J. F. L. Rolleston, M.P.	1	1	0	,, Healey Street house ...	2	18	6
Major Stanhope Rolleston	1	0	0	,, Irlam Street house	1	1	6
Mr. W. Freeman	0	5	0	Pocket money for Blaby Road house ...	1	0	0
Miss Bumpstead	0	10	0	,, ,, Healey Street house ...	0	17	0
Arnesby Main Street Baptist C. E. Society	0	10	6	Railway Fares and Season Tickets ...	3	14	1
South Wigston Congregational Sunday School (two collections) ...	0	7	7	Clothing and Boots	2	5	10
Collection made in Station Street ...	0	3	0	Boot Repairs	0	18	3
South Wigston Boys' School (five colls.)	0	14	11½	Printing, Memo Books, etc. ...	0	10	9
St. Thomas' Church, South Wigston (per Mr. E. Veasey) ...	2	15	11		60	17	11½
Collected by Mr. Johnson's Dog ("Kelly")	0	3	0½	Cash in hand... ... 5 13 2½			
South Wigston Shoe Works	1	4	3	Balance in Bank 60 16 3			
Box Factory (three collections)	0	15	0		66	9	5½
Mid. Rly. Loco. Dept. (per Mr. Kenney) four collections	4	3	11				
Subscriptions :—							
Mr. J. W. Black, C.C.	14	6	0				
,, A. W. Bruce	1	10	0				
,, W. Parker	1	5	0				
,, J. T. Moore, U.D.C. ...	0	16	6				
Miss A. Geeves	0	13	0				
Amount collected by house-to-house collection	69	4	5½				
Bank Interest	0	1	3				
	£127	7	5		£127	7	5

First Quarter Balance Sheet for the South Wigston and Glen Parva Belgian Relief Fund. (*Wigston and District Free Churchman*, March 1915)

By March 1915, South Wigston and Glen Parva had established a separate Belgian Refugee Fund whose chairman was Arthur William Bruce of Fernleigh House, Glen Parva. Bruce was a partner in Bruce & Sons, Brunswick Works, Garden Street, South Wigston, an elastic-web manufacturing company. This Refugee Fund had raised £127 7s 5d in its first quarter and was renting three properties situated in Healey Street, Irlam Street and at No. 27 Blaby Road. A note in the Wigston Magna Urban District Council minutes records that the occupant of the latter home during 1916 and 1917, and probably longer, was M. Leribaux.

There were many efforts made to help the Belgians settle. Some examples in Leicester included a reception and dinner held at the Museum in New Walk, hosted by the Mayor, Jonathan North. He was Chairman of Freeman, Hardy & Willis Ltd., and was later knighted for service to Leicester as Mayor, a position he held throughout the entire conflict. *The Leicester Daily Mercury* printed a regular column of mainly Belgian news in the Flemish language, and in South Wigston the local Conservative Club offered free membership to Belgian residents.

Some Belgians moved their accommodation or returned home before the end of the war. Certainly those at The Grange left early because, during 1916, Albert Edward Hill and his family are recorded as living there (he went on to buy the property from the Tyler family in 1922). However, most of the refugees remained until after the Armistice was signed, but even then there were delays. *The Leicester Daily Mercury* of 13 February 1919 reported:

It is probable that within a few days arrangements will be completed for the repatriation of all Belgian refugees in Leicester and Leicestershire. M/s A.E. Bouchout, secretary of the local Belgian Bureau, who is acting on behalf of the Belgian authorities has received a telegram from the Local Government Board requesting him to 'wire' the number of refugees in the borough and county, and to send embarkation returns at once.

The paper continued on 15 February 1919:

Worries by the Belgians anxious to return and the British worried about unemployment and housing shortage were both wondering what was the delay in their repatriation ... the situation in Belgium is not good for sending back large numbers all at once. Food, transport and housing being the chief obstacle ... Strikes at various works in England during the last two months have very seriously delayed the programme ... Difficulty of getting ships repaired and despatched ... sections of British workers responsible for the hold-up were not acting in a very sportsmanlike spirit towards dependents of men who have been their comrades in the field for years past, towards the

Blaby Road, South Wigston with Countesthorpe Road on the right. Number 27 Blaby Road is one of the shop premises beyond the turn, now a health and beauty parlour. (Tricia Berry)

gallant and brave nation which, whilst holding the road at Leige prevented England from being invaded and that 'the unions' might at least see that refugees should not be put to this serious inconvenience … withdrawal of Allied Troops, British and French, from Belgium is steadily relieving the food position … railway authorities have now been able to resume their activities … and accommodation is being provided for the unfortunate people whom invasion had driven from their own country, and who had been stripped of everything, including dwellings and furniture.

Eight hundred will leave Leicester in two trains about the 25th with luggage for Hull … Shipping arrangements made by the Local Government Board and local arrangements by the Belgian Bureau … British Government offer of free repatriation is provided through local police … When date of sailing is known an authority card to facilitate checking by rail and shipping authorities … also to act as an Identity Card on arrival on native soil and allow free transport on Belgian railways … could take up to 300lbs of luggage including 28lbs of food (up to 2lbs of coffee), per head. M/s Bouchout would escort the party to Hull … journey to Antwerp … two days. It is hoped that Leicestershire and Rutland people who for four years have been interested in local Belgian guests and shown them every kindness … will give them a hearty send off and say God speed on their journey.

The Belgians came, and went, leaving little accessible information about themselves. The Leicester ones did, however, present a beautiful painting, *Britannia with Belgian Refugees*, to Leicester Museum Service, and created a booklet of poems to express gratitude to their hosts, which is held within the local Record Office collections. One other reminder, the retired Belgian police detective, Hercule Poirot, who features in Agatha Christie's novels, was based on a Belgian refugee.

5

WILLIAM EWART BOULTER VC AND HIS BAND OF BROTHERS

BY DEREK SEATON

William Ewart Boulter was born at No. 51 Bull Head Street, Wigston Magna, Leicestershire, on 14 October 1892. His parents were Fred and Mary Ann Boulter. Fred was born in Wigston Magna on 2 August 1866 whilst Mary Ann Boulter (née Dore) came from the tiny village of Dunton Bassett, 3½ miles from Lutterworth in Leicestershire, where she was born on Christmas Eve 1864.

Fred Boulter and Mary Ann Dore were married at the Independent Chapel in Long Street, Wigston Magna, on 4 August 1890 by the Revd T. Cope Deeming. Fred's occupation was shown as a rotary hand and his wife was employed as a domestic servant.

The young couple's first child, George, was born in late 1890 followed by William Ewart in October 1892. On William's birth certificate his father's occupation was recorded as a stocking framework-knitter.

Further additions to the Boulter family came with the birth of Albert on 24 June 1894 and Harold on 14 July 1896. Finally, a longed-for daughter, Mabel, was born in 1898 and then another girl, Sarah May, on 11 May 1904.

The young William Boulter commenced his education at Bell Street Infants' School, situated in the heart of the community. Known to all his contemporaries as Billy he made many new friends. He was popular and well liked; team games and sporting activities he found particularly appealing and participated in with relish. He duly moved on from the Infants' School to Great Wigston Board School in Long Street.

It was here that the young Billy Boulter spent his formative years. He became renowned for his sporting prowess and was particularly successful at both association football and cricket. In 1904 he left Long Street School, aged 12 years.

Upon leaving school he commenced work with the Wigston Co-operative Stores Ltd as a grocer's assistant in the village shop. William's next move, in late 1911, was to join the Leicester Co-operative Society Ltd., where he secured a position in the drapery department situated in the huge store in High Street, Leicester, which was opened in 1884 and extended in 1910.

Meanwhile, the head of the Boulter family, Fred, had emerged as a leading figure in the rapidly developing Wigston Hosiery Society, an Industrial Co-operative that had been established in 1897. He became the factory manager in 1909 and went on to oversee the building of a replacement factory, described as 'a fine new building', in Paddock Street, during 1913.

In the furtherance of his own career, and whilst remaining in the employment of the Co-operative Society, Billy Boulter moved to Kettering in 1912 to take up a position with the Kettering Industrial Co-operative Society Ltd. He secured a position as an assistant at the Society's drapery department in Newland Street, Kettering.

He quickly settled into his new life in the pleasant Northamptonshire town and integrated easily and fully into the local community. During his stay in Kettering he lodged with Henry and Elizabeth Shuffle at their home at No. 38 Princes Street, just a short walk from his place of work in Newland Street.

Life in many ways was idyllic and carefree as 1914 dawned, but all was about to change as war clouds in Europe appeared on the horizon. Soon, the lives of Billy and his young friends were to be changed forever. The tranquillity of the English summer was shattered on Tuesday, 4 August 1914 when it was announced that Britain had declared war on Germany. A week later, Kitchener's recruitment campaign was everywhere, with his ominous finger pointing at all potential recruits.

In Northamptonshire, along with every other county and city throughout Britain, young men flocked to the recruiting offices to answer the call of King and Country. William Boulter, along with six of his friends from the Kettering Thursday Football Club, enlisted in the town on 4 September 1914.

He was aged 21 years and 11 months on enlistment. His medical details were recorded as follows:

Height	5ft 6¼in
Weight	131lbs (9 stone 5lbs)
Chest	35in girth when fully expanded
Measurements expanded	2¼in range of expansion

Private Boulter was allocated his service number – 14603 – and posted the following day to the 6th (Service) Battalion, The Northamptonshire Regiment, known and respected throughout the British Army as 'The Steelbacks'.

The 6th (Service) Battalion was one of three service battalions (5th, 6th and 7th) raised by The Northamptonshire Regiment in response to Kitchener's recruitment campaign. Along with hundreds of newly formed Service Battalions throughout the country, they became known as Kitchener's Army or K's men. The first Commanding Officer of the 6th Northamptonshires was Lieutenant-Colonel George Eustace Ripley, a veteran of the Boer War who came out of retirement to answer his country's call.

Initially the 6th (Service) Battalion, The Northamptonshire Regiment, was stationed at Shorncliffe Camp, Cheriton, in Kent, where they became one of the units that comprised the 18th (Eastern) Division of the Second New Army, made up of men from the southern and eastern counties, under the command of Major-General (Frederick) Ivor Maxse. The Division, which had three Brigades contained Service Battalions from thirteen infantry Regiments.

Throughout twelve months of vigorous training at Shorncliffe, Colchester and at Codford St Mary on Salisbury Plain to prepare the battalion for the Western Front, William Boulter's service record makes interesting reading:

Rank	Date
Attested Private	4 September 1914
Appointed (paid) Lance-Corporal	29 September 1914
Promoted Corporal	18 November 1914
Appointed (paid) Lance-Sergeant	13 April 1915

The 6th Northamptonshires were moved to France and onwards to the Western Front in July 1915. Lance-Sergeant Boulter had rapidly developed his skills as an infantryman with a command of all of the weapons he was required to use in action, particularly the machine-gun and Mills bomb (No. 5). In addition he possessed the gift of leadership and, as a senior NCO, won the respect of his subordinates.

Despite a less than satisfactory company conduct sheet, which contained entries all centred upon his bizarre and unacceptable levels of timekeeping, Sergeant Boulter was considered by his superiors to be one who, when he was most needed on the field of battle, would not be found wanting. This assessment was to be prophetic indeed!

Action was first encountered during August when the 18th Division took over part of the front line in the Somme area and was engaged in a sector which included Carnoy and Marmetz. There was little intensive fighting in the division's allocated area at this particular time, thus the new battalions were able to acclimatise gradually and to gain in confidence in their early days in the trenches.

Sergeant William Ewart Boulter VC. (Jeremy Birkett)

On 26 July 1915, Lance-Sergeant Boulter was promoted to the rank of Sergeant.

Following the commencement of the Battle of the Somme on 1 July 1916, with its catastrophic casualty rates, the British High Command devised a bold plan to launch an attack on the German second-line defences situated to the south of the Allied Front on the Somme. The strategic objective was the taking of the Bazentin Ridge, which involved the capture of three villages and a number of heavily defended woods.

The plan for this daring attack, in which troops would assemble during the hours of darkness, was master-minded by Lieutenant-General Sir Henry Rawlinson who commanded the British Fourth Army.

Four divisions were earmarked for a surprise dawn offensive in addition to which a single and strategic objective was allocated to Major-General Maxse's 18th Division. This was the taking and holding of Trones Wood, which occupied a critical position on the extreme right of the attacking force. It was vital to capture the wood in its entirety to protect the right flank of the attacking force and before the main attack commenced on 14 July.

The initial attack on the evening of 13 July was repulsed. Major-General Maxse responded by ordering a second attack for which two battalions were selected, the 6th (Service) Battalion, The Northamptonshire Regiment, and the 12th (Service) Battalion, The Middlesex Regiment. Stiff resistance was encountered and mounting casualties were being taken as the two battalions, under the overall command of Lieutenant-Colonel Frank Maxwell VC, DSO, the commanding officer of the 12th Middlesex, edged their way forward in a line, sweeping towards the northern apex of the wood.

The greatest danger was posed at a point where the wood narrowed and there was an area of open ground in front of a German machine-gun post that was inflicting heavy casualties. By this time Sergeant Boulter had taken command of his platoon following the loss of all of his officers. He quickly assessed the situation and seized the initiative.

Single-handedly he charged the machine-gun post, with his bag of bombs, in the face of withering fire. He zig-zagged his way towards the machine gun and during this daring feat of bravery he was shot through the left shoulder by a German sniper. Despite being severely wounded he was able, by means of his skill as a grenade thrower, sheer athleticism and raw indefinable courage, to bomb the enemy gun team from their position and remove the deadly threat to his advancing comrades.

Sergeant Boulter finally fell exhausted within 20 yards of the machine gun. After a few minutes he managed to get to his feet again. Although bleeding profusely and in considerable pain, he walked back unaided to the nearest dressing station, over 2,000 yards behind the line, for urgent medical attention.

With the elimination of the remaining machine gun by Sergeant Boulter, Trones Wood was finally cleared and was entirely in the hands of the 18th Division. By the end of the day the attack on the Bazentin Ridge had proved to be a significant success.

The 6th Battalion, The Northamptonshire Regiment, suffered heavy casualties in the taking of the wood.

Killed	36
Wounded	204
Missing	35
Shell Shock	7
Total Casualties	282

With the exception of Major Sidney Herbert Charrington, the temporary commanding officer, and two young subalterns, all the remaining officers had been killed or wounded.

The 5th Northern General Hospital, Leicester. (Derek Seaton)

On Sunday, 16 July, Sergeant Boulter was on his way back to England. The hospital ship landed at Southampton the following day and he was admitted to hospital there. On 19 July he was transferred to Litchfield Military Hospital where he received surgical treatment to his badly injured left shoulder. From 7 September to 21 October he was a patient at the 5th Northern General Hospital, Leicester (now the Fielding Johnson building of the University of Leicester).

He was then discharged to the British Red Cross Society Hospital at Belper for a period of convalescence from where he proceeded on sick leave to the family home at No. 9 Central Avenue, Wigston Magna.

By October 1916, Fred and Mary Boulter had three of their four sons serving in the British Army. Albert had enlisted into The Leicestershire Regiment and was serving with the 2nd Battalion in Mesopotamia. A skilled marksman, he was deployed as a sniper. Harold, the youngest of the brothers, joined the Royal Army Medical Corps on 29 October 1915, having volunteered at the age of 19 years. He was stationed in England at the time.

The Boulter family had good reason to be proud of the contribution their boys were making for King and Country but suddenly, and quite unexpectedly, their level of pride was to know no bounds. On Thursday, 26 October, whilst having dinner with his family, a telegram arrived informing Sergeant Boulter that he had been awarded the Victoria Cross. The news caused great elation within the family, their neighbours and friends and throughout Wigston Magna.

A prestigious list of fifteen recipients of the Victoria Cross had been published in the Fourth Supplement to *The London Gazette* (24 October 1916).

The individual citations were given in detail and, in the case of Sergeant Boulter, his citation read:

No 14603 Sergeant William Ewart Boulter, Northamptonshire Regiment For most conspicuous bravery. When one company and part of another were held up in the attack on a wood by a hostile machine-gun, which was causing heavy casualties, Sergeant Boulter, with utter contempt of danger and in spite of being severely wounded in the shoulder, advanced alone and over the open ground under heavy fire in front of the gun, and bombed the gun team from their position.

This very gallant act not only saved many casualties, but was of great military value, as it materially expedited the operation of clearing the enemy out of the wood, and thus covering the flank of the whole attacking force.

23766 Private Albert Boulter, 2nd Battalion, The Leicestershire Regiment.
(Mrs Marion Partridge)

As the news of William Boulter's award spread, the family home was besieged by newspaper reporters and photographers. As he struggled to regain his composure, he was almost overwhelmed with invitations to attend receptions to be held in his honour at Wigston Magna, Kettering and Northampton.

In an impressive reception at Northampton on Saturday, 4 November 1916 it was estimated that 20,000 people assembled in Abington Park to greet him.

The final public reception for Sergeant Boulter took place, appropriately, in his own village of Wigston Magna in Leicestershire, on Saturday, 9 December. He was invited, together with his parents, his younger sister Sarah May and his fiancée Florence May Lusher to receive the acclamations of those who lived in the place where his father's family had their roots.

103331 Private Harold Boulter, Royal Army Medical Corps. (Mrs Eileen Vann)

Sergeant William Ewart Boulter VC photographed with his parents and fiancée, together with local dignitaries, at a public reception in his honour, which took place at Wigston Magna on 9 December 1916. *(Leicester Mercury)*

A temporary platform consisted of a cart belonging to Councillor Eli Bailey, a carter and farmer and a member of the Wigston Magna Urban District Council. The event was described in the *Illustrated Leicester Chronicle* accompanied by a splendid photograph of the occasion.

On 17 March 1917, Sergeant Boulter attended an investiture at Buckingham Palace where His Majesty King George V decorated him with the Victoria Cross. He was, by this time, an Officer Cadet striving to obtain the King's Commission and on 24 July, having successfully completed his training at No. 13 Officer Cadet Battalion at Newmarket, he was gazetted as a Temporary 2nd Lieutenant.

Meanwhile George, the eldest of the Boulter brothers, had been conscripted into the Royal Navy. He had been employed in a key position at the Wigston Hosiery Society's factory where his father was the manager. George was in charge of the making-up of the garments during a period of intense activity with Government contracts to be fulfilled and huge demands being made upon the workforce.

Conscription was introduced as a result of the Military Service Act 1916 and eventually George had to leave his post, important though it was in terms of the war effort, in order to follow his brothers into the forces. George joined the Royal Navy on 8 August 1917 and did his initial training on HMS *Victory*. At that time, Admiral Horatio Nelson's famous flagship was afloat off Gosport and was the flagship of Admiral The Honourable Sir Stanley Colville, Commander-in-Chief, Portsmouth.

Having received his commission, 2nd Lieutenant William Boulter VC was posted to the 7th (Service) Battalion, The Northamptonshire Regiment, and returned to France to join his new battalion who were engaged in the Third Battle of Ypres (Passchendaele). His involvement

P/J75666 Ordinary Seaman George Boulter. (Mrs Marion Partridge)

with the 7th Battalion was shortlived, as it became necessary for him to be withdrawn from active service on 16 October upon suffering from trench fever and acute bronchitis. Following a prolonged period of medical treatment he was finally released from the Army on 25 April 1919 with the rank of Lieutenant.

By the end of 1919 the Boulter family was once again united in that, amazingly, all of Fred and Mary's four sons had survived the war and had returned home from the various theatres of war across the world. George, the eldest, was demobilised from the Royal Navy on 7 July 1919. Albert, who was wounded whilst serving in Mesopotamia, had moved with the 2nd Battalion, The Leicestershire Regiment, to India from where he eventually returned home.

Harold Boulter served in Mesopotamia from 25 December 1916 to 31 December 1918 before leaving for Russia with his unit on 1 January 1919. He was eventually demobilised on 19 November 1919. Upon discharge he was suffering from malaria fever but eventually overcame his illness.

The proud service record of the Boulter family can be summarised as follows:

Name	Services	Theatres of War	Wounded etc.	Gallantry
George	Royal Navy	Scapa Flow		
William Ewart	The North-amptonshire Regiment	Belgium/France	Wounded	Awarded the Victoria Cross
Albert	The Leicestershire Regiment	Mesopotamia/India	Wounded	
Harold	Royal Army Medical Corps	Mesopotamia/Russia	Malaria	

The Boulter family's response to the Call to Arms, like so many other families, had been immense, unquestioned and viewed as their contribution to King and Country in time of war. William Ewart Boulter VC and his fighting brothers are remembered with pride and gratitude in their native village of Wigston Magna.

6

THE WAR EFFORT
BY JEAN DANN

Local manufacturing firms appeared to do well during the war years with many hosiery companies supplying the army with woollen clothing. Some took the decision to increase their workers' wages, even so, the cost of living for ordinary people escalated over time. It was felt by many that too much money was spent on alcohol but without doubt the generosity of Wigston people to give to local charities was astounding.

At the beginning of autumn 1914 a large working party was held in the Co-operative Hall in Long Street each Tuesday. The group had been formed to make items for the Red Cross (as long as funds allowed the work continued).

The Co-operative Hall (right) on Long Street, Wigston Magna. (Duncan Lucas)

Donations for materials had been given by the local community; money came from individuals and local chapels. Friends of the Primitive Methodist Church gave 5s 6d, the Wesleyan Methodist Church 15s. Business and professional people donating included: J.D. Broughton, £1; Dr and Mrs Longford, 5s; Mr Foulston, 2s 6d; Mrs A Shipp, 2s 6d; Charles Lewin, 10s; and Doctor Briggs, 10s; Mrs Ladkin, 2s 6d; Mr and Mrs A Hill, £1; Mr and Mrs T Goodin, 2s 6d; Mrs Mortlock, 5s; and Mrs Owston, £3.

It was reported that Miss Brown and her bible class were also knitting hard for the Red Cross. A collection at All Saints' Church had raised £11 14s for the Prince of Wales National Fund. The fund was used for families dependent upon serving soldiers. The young Prince of Wales, later the Duke of Windsor, was treasurer and a photo postcard of him as a young man was sold in aid of the charity with half a penny donation from each sale.

By 25 September 1914, Revd Wright reported to his parishioners that the people of Wigston had raised a total of £400 for the Prince of Wales Fund. The Belgian Relief Fund had raised £10 from a concert at the Co-operative Hall and £9 10s from an appeal in the parish magazine.

 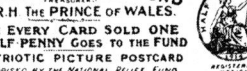

Postcard of His Royal Highness the Prince of Wales sold in aid of the National Relief Fund. (Jean Dann)

A letter printed in a chapel magazine congratulated the people of Wigston on their support in raising money for the Prince of Wales Fund and the Red Cross. By this time the Red Cross Working Party had made and sent nearly 600 garments to the sick and wounded and had collected over £40 for the materials used: £11 had been collected during a band parade led by their well-known South Wigston bandmaster Charlie Moore.

In October 1914, Revd Wright said that some of his church members, Messrs Ross, Quincey and Hancock, had been promoted to the rank of Colour Sergeant, whilst Messrs Bernard Brewin and Horton had been made Corporals. He continued: 'The winter dances and entertainments will hardly seem

Charles Moore, Bandmaster, Choirmaster and Conductor. (Janice Broughton)

possible at such times of sadness. I can't help personally hoping that such will not be arranged. I hope that money people usually spend will be given to the Belgian Fund instead. It seems to me that none should be playing football or paying to watch it except those who have been rejected at recruiting stations.'

By 22 October 1914 the number of garments made by the Red Cross Working Party had reached 700. Miss Brown's senior girls' bible class had completed work for the Base Hospital in Leicester and a balance of 20s had been passed on to the local Belgian Relief Fund.

January's fundraising continued at a pace and by 27 January 1915 All Saints' parish magazine reported that various classes had raised funds – Mr Gardener's class 21s for the Belgian Relief Fund, Miss Brown's class, coffee and butter weekly, also for the Belgian Fund. A parcel of woollen jerseys was made and sent to the men of the navy and a parcel of woollen comforters to the Base Hospital.

All Saints' Church choir gave up their yearly treat, and the proceeds of a Mothers' Meeting tea amounted to £1 10s for the Belgian Relief Fund. Following a successful sale, the Girl Guides bought wool to make articles for the wounded. South Wigston Methodist Church received an appeal from the Queen's Work for Women Fund but delayed any decision to take part until the following year.

As summer arrived, Wigston's fundraising for the war effort was in overdrive. By 27 May 1915 the church day schools had collected and contributed £1 2s to the Children's Hat Fund for Soldiers; £3 9s 6d to the National Sailors Society; £1 to Soldiers Luxuries Fund, and 10s 6d to the Sand Bag Fund. A fund box was put out during All Saints' School tea and treat, so that the children could drop in pennies for comforts for soldiers: 2s 6d was raised and given to the wounded at Glen Parva Barracks.

In June, the list of old boys and teachers from the All Saints' Church School who had joined the Army or Navy was so large that a second tablet had been required and inscribed by Mr Herrick. At South Wigston Wesleyan Church a roll of honour was read out that contained over thirty names.

On Thursday 1 July 1915 a special fundraising Café Chantant event took place in the grounds of St Thomas' vicarage garden. Tickets were 1s each and proceeds were in aid of the Red Cross Ambulance Transport for wounded soldiers in Leicester. It was reported that so far eleven stretcher vans had been purchased, each van taking four stretcher cases to the Base Hospital or North Evington. Debt on the vans was still £300 in addition to upkeep and petrol. Later in the month smaller events were taking place, including a whist drive and strawberry tea in aid of wounded soldiers and the local voluntary aid detachment. Wounded soldiers had been entertained in Wigston by the Girls' Communicant Guild in the grounds of local businessman J.D. Broughton.

Revd Wright commented: 'There have been many other entertainments such as band parades and carnivals whether these things are suitable for these sad times I don't know, I personally don't feel in tune with them right now.'

Also in July, the South Wigston Conservative Club announced that they were starting up a subscription list to save towards parcels for their seven members serving at the front. These were sent the following month to the value of 3s each. It was also decided to purchase a photo frame to contain photos of members and members' sons serving with the colours. Also proposed was that members could invite Belgian Refugees and any soldiers staying in the locality for any length of time to become temporary members.

On Monday 16 August, forty-five wounded soldiers were entertained at the National School with tea and various musical events, including music by the Mellowe's Orchestral Band. Miss Carrie Sampson presented each soldier with a buttonhole, grapes, chocolate, cigarettes and lemonade. They were later returned to hospital in motor cars which in itself was an event. Later that month the teachers of the church school, old scholars and girls of the first class organised an Emblem Day in aid of a permanent holiday home for disabled soldiers at Lowestoft and collected 27 guineas. Each guinea enabled a Wigston disabled soldier to take a fortnight's holiday at Lowestoft.

All Saints' Church School, Long Street, Wigston Magna. (Duncan Lucas)

At their meeting on 17 September, South Wigston Conservative Club decided to give 5s towards the Carnival Fund in aid of serving Wigston soldiers.

Moat Street Primitive Methodists held a 'Grand Complimentary Concert to the Wounded Soldiers of his Majesty's Army'. The concert, held on Monday 6 September, was a programme of songs, duets and recitals. Programmes were sold for 6d each. The itinerary of twelve items included recitals by the Misses Hincks, Miss Johnson sang 'Till the Boys Come Home', Mr Payne sang 'The Drum Major', and all were accompanied by Violet Moore.

South Wigston Methodists decided that in the event of any teacher or Sunday School scholar having to leave the church to join the Army or Navy they should be sent a bible when they reached the age of 21. This would have been the case if they were at home.

A 'Flag Day for Serbian Relief' was held which yielded £66 17s 9d, and later the British Red Cross Society also held a 'Flag Day', theirs raising the large sum of £100.

One wonders if employers were taking advantage of women employees as cheap labour. Revd Wright points out in his monthly letter in January 1916 his concern about inequalities between rich and poor particularly the 'sweated wage' earned by women. He says:

I heard of such a wage the other day, a woman using her own machine and supplying her own thread is making one dozen pairs of the upper parts of a boot – that is 24 'uppers' and each upper is made up of ten separate pieces of material including the lining, all of which have to be sewn together, and on each upper there are nine buttons to be sewn on – and what do you think she got paid for this? The glorious sum of one shilling and sixpence for making 24 uppers; and if the size of the boot was a small one she got paid one shilling and threepence.

Outdoor working was common place for women in the Wigston area and remained so for many years.

Raising money for the war effort continued into the new year. The Girl Guides had contributed almost £20 to the War Funds since the beginning of the war and an auction and variety sale was planned for 2 March in aid of the Leicestershire Nursing Association Emergency Home at No. 6 Blaby Road, South Wigston.

The Boy Scouts were in debt for outfits and rents for their room in Bell Street and were hoping to have a fundraising event to cover these. Some of the older scouts were serving on coastal-defence work.

Also that month an unusual gift was presented to All Saints' Church. A crucifix was given by Mr Howe of Central Avenue from the ruins of a church in Belgium. Mr Howe felt that the parish church was the right place for it and when peace came again it could be returned if it was asked for.

Primitive Methodist Chapel, Moat Street, Wigston Magna. (Duncan Lucas)

In July, a memorial service was held at All Saints' Church for all men who had fallen in war. Wigston had lost about twenty men so far, the last post was sounded. The church had provided a 'War Corner' and Revd Wright was hoping for a permanent memorial in the North Aisle and asked for donations to fund it.

It was reported that Wigston men who were prisoners of war in Germany would be sent parcels from the Leicestershire Prisoners of War Society. The cost for parcels each month was £10 16s. A local resident, Miss Pochin, represented the fund in Wigston and was keen for more subscriptions. Sadly by the end of the year Miss Pochin had died and the fund had lost its most loyal supporter.

In September it had been decided that all war charities had to be registered under the War Charities Act 1916. One of the first to register was the South Wigston and Glen Parva Wounded Soldiers Tea Committee. The sum of 12s was given to the fund by the South Wigston Conservative Club.

Following on from their successful concert the previous year, Moat Street Primitive Methodists held another concert on Monday 4 September, again entitled 'Grand Complimentary Concert to the Wounded Soldiers of His Majesty's Army'. A different selection of twelve songs, duets and recitals was given. Dr Briggs gave a recitation called 'Bill Adams', Florence Hincks a musical monologue, Miss Green sang 'Laddie in Khaki' and Violet Moore was again their accompanist.

At this time money was fairly plentiful at the Wigston Hosiers in Paddock Street. Government orders were abundant and wages were increased accordingly. In addition to their staff numbers new employees would need to be available from the 'non eligible' list. The society's thoughts were with its members serving at the front. Their army pay was increased and a Christmas parcel to the value of 5s was sent to every absent member. Throughout the war years, the Wigston Hosiers gave a considerable amount of money to various war charities.

During 1917 the Mayor of Leicester wanted to raise £100,000 for the support of disabled soldiers and sailors and asked the local Council if they would like to become involved with the project. If a sum of £600 could be raised locally then Wigston men could benefit from the scheme.

The Council appeared to be unlucky with their horses, as one of them was again commandeered by the Government – it had only been purchased the year before. However, this time they were paid £90 towards its replacement. The council grew oats for their working horses on the land around the sewerage works and the following year was able to put 20 tons of oat straw up for auction.

The Local Government Board required urgent help for further systematic collection of waste paper, scrap metal, glass and woollen and cotton articles, it was hoped the Boy Scouts would take up the challenge.

By 1918 the war had impacted on most people, manufacturers and institutions in Wigston. One local institution was the Almshouses in Long Street which was overseen by a group of trustees. Each of their meetings was headed up by the date and extent of the war, for example '22 May 1918 and the 4th year and 292 days of the Great War'. At this particular meeting they welcomed home one of their members, Colonel Parker, who had been away on active service for three years during which he had served some of the time in Mesopotamia. Another of their members, Mr M. Buszard, was still in Siam and wouldn't return until June 1919.

The Council reported that two large concerts were to be arranged in Wigston Magna and another in South Wigston for Saturday 15 June, open air if possible, all the proceeds to go to St Dunstan's who provided care and rehabilitation for blind soldiers. These eventually raised £58 7s 0d.

By July it was reported that Wigston had thirty men who were prisoners of war. Revd Wright later reported to his parishioners on 30 August 1918 that two Wigston funds, the Sailors and Soldiers Christmas Parcel Fund and the Prisoners of War Fund, continued to be supported. A sum of £100 had been raised chiefly from a sports event held on 5 August. However, he felt that another £300 would be needed before Christmas if all the men were to receive presents.

The Almshouses, Long Street, Wigston Magna. (Duncan Lucas)

The Prisoners of War Fund raised over £100 by a garden fête and dance, but he felt again that much more would be needed for the duration of the war. He went on to say that he was chairman of both the Benevolent Fund and the Parcels Fund, each of which were in need of extra money. The Benevolent Fund distributed £50 in the previous year for relief of sick cases in Wigston, however it was presently without money and was having to borrow to continue its good work.

By September 1918 the Leicestershire Discharged Sailors and Soldiers Federation Wigston Branch had secured the old Parish Room in Bushloe End as a 'Recreation Hut' but it required furnishing. Continuing with local generosity, several people offered furnishings. The secretary was Mr W. Lynn, of No. 87 Leicester Road. It was hoped that this would lead to a more permanent building for when the men returned home.

Alan Kind, a long-standing resident of South Wigston, summed up the feelings of people in South Wigston in 1918:

Whilst there was an air of expectation the fact that many would not return was a sobering thought. There was a feeling of anger at the carnage the war had caused and to what end? Some families were without their bread winners. Years would pass before the horror of what many had endured could be told. My father, Orson, joined up in 1915 and saw active service in Mesopotamia and was later wounded in the Battle of Kut-el-Amara in 1916. He returned home but rarely mentioned his experiences. Clearly, the old order had to change but regretfully it took another worldwide conflict to bring this about.

7

1914 WARTIME
BY DUNCAN LUCAS

Frank Noble, a South Wigston lad, loaned me his school book and allowed me to copy it and, by golly, as the years roll on, it gains significance.

It is recorded as Transaction 51 of the Greater Wigston Historical Society. It tells of Kitchener's blue-coated volunteers sleeping in front gardens and houses, and of the turmoil of a war time garrison town.

My memories flow because as a lad I worked in the fields, in threshing gangs, absorbing the yarns and tales almost as if I'd been there.

We worked a grand old horse called Bob during 1939–42 who was a 1914/1918 veteran. He had an army brand, and when working up Aylestone Lane and the bugles played at Glen Parva Barracks, half a mile as the crow flies, his ears would prick up and a snort or two would emanate. Uncle Les told that the loss of a horse caused an enquiry because it cost £20. A soldier? Well he cost the King's 1/-.

Whilst on the subject of horses, a soldier leading his horses to water them fell down exhausted. The lead horse sniffed him, carefully stepped over him and went on to drink. Affinity between man and horse.

Of the mule which was made untameable until a Mexican (how did he get to France?) mounted the mule, rode it at a wall again and again until the mule stood still a mass of trembling. The best horsemanship ever seen I was told.

Bert Fisher of the bored cavalry men who were kept in reserve who caught cats stuffed them head first into a cavalry long boot and castrated them. Fun. Sick! Well the world around was. Or the soldier waggoner who could shoot and kill a hare at long range. He would share his spoils on condition that his skill was not reported. He preferred his wagon to the hell of a sniper in the trenches.

Of the raiding of an orchard and the soldiers returning to billets with masses of rosy red apples, only one man, Les Forryan the farm lad, picked the

Private Leslie Hedges Forryan, Army Service Corps and two army horses. (Duncan Lucas)

plain ones! It was a cider orchard and the red apples were bitter. The plain ones were sweet!

Mrs Proctor, who had a sweet shop and recounted many local legends to us small boys, told of how she obtained a sugar allowance to make her special slab toffee and of her nephew Melvin Strachan (Proctor?) who died in Mesopotamia, and whose name is on a gravestone in Wigston Cemetery. Research shows him as the Deputy Chief Fireman of the Wigston Fire Brigade prior to joining the army.

Father told of rum rations being flashed around before going over the top. Half of us were drunk he said, otherwise we would not have gone. He told us when we were kids, he would not have any 'Trickers' jams or products in the house. He suffered Trickers plum and apple jam in the trenches – it was put on cheese not bread to bind the stomach up. The company had the contract to supply the army but post war their reputation killed them.

Pop told of a cemetery shelled and corpses sitting on the trees with their night caps on. He insisted on his own cremation as the sight never left him, of a dentist in his company who collected special jars of teeth from body parts.

Of Germans shouting over trenches 'don't shoot we are your brothers, Hanoverians or Saxons'. So we didn't shoot. It was peaceful but the generals didn't like it so we were moved. The French came in and battle recommenced.

THE AFTERMATH

Jack Mills had a saw mill on the end of Junction Road and Mill Lane where he prepared logs and sticks for sale. He had lost a leg, or was it both, but he got around in his pony and trap. A wonderful bass singer, when I took the milk round, I often head him practising for some concert or other.

Ethel Howe of tennis-court fame on Aylestone Lane was courting a sailor who was killed. Ethel only married very late in her life but on her death I was given some handmade baby clothes which she had made in preparation of marriage and family. They are now in Snibston Museum.

Families who lost loved ones received citations etc., and Mrs Mawby in Bull Head Street, a war widow, kept a mini shrine until her death in the 1960s.

Peter Percy Parsons who lived in Junction Road was a carver of artificial limbs for the wounded. Mr Windridge kept a fancy goods shop on Leicester Road – he had only one eye. Another Mr Windridge lived on Horsewell Lane. I never saw him out of a wheelchair. He had lost a leg, or was it both. I never knew, but he had a large family.

Here Charlie Debraux bragged that he had 3 sons despite losing a testicle in the Somme. We told him he had a zealous milkman!

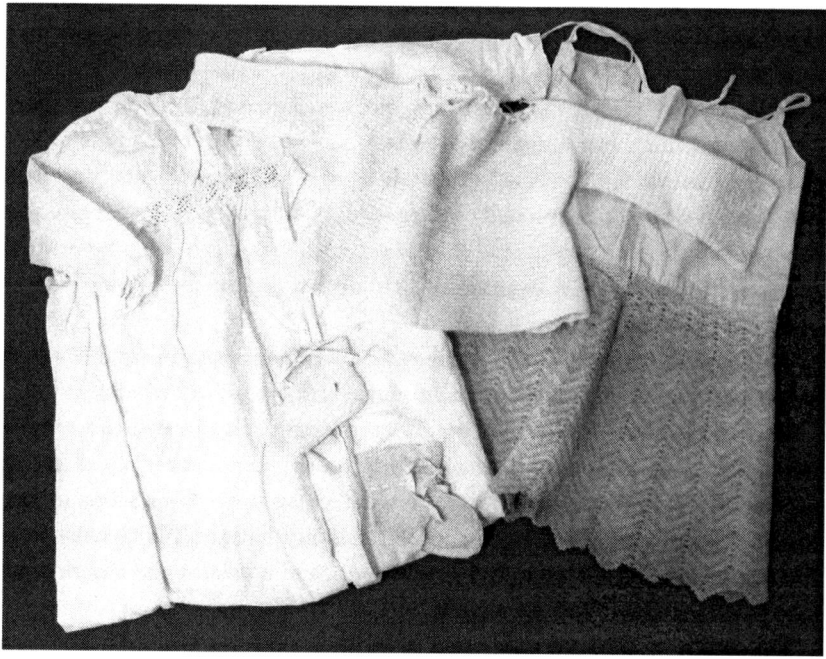

Baby clothes made by Ethel Howe. (Snibston Discovery Park)

Then Jack Holland who died aged 95 with shrapnel still in his body. He was registered dead in the battle but his sergeant went to pay his last respects in the field hospital and noticed a movement. He fetched help and Jack lasted till his 90s. His tag had been removed and he was a declared dead and so his name appeared on a war memorial (Cosby) despite his long life.

Another soldier who survived serious injuries from shrapnel wounds was 202043 Sergeant Arthur Snow who served in The Northamptonshire Regiment. He was born in nearby Blaby on 29 April 1897 but later moved to Wigston Magna where he spent the greater part of his life.

Initially, Arthur Snow enlisted into the 4th Battalion, The Leicestershire Regiment on 26 October 1915 and subsequently transferred to the 3/4th Battalion, The Northamptonshire Regiment on 10 July 1916 at his own request: 'For the purpose of serving with his elder brother' under King's Regulations 333. His brother Edward was a senior NCO serving with the Northamptons at that time. Later Arthur served with the 4th (Reserve) Battalion and finally the 6th (Service) Battalion. [The same battalion in which Sergeant William Ewart Boulter VC had served earlier – *see* chapter 5.]

Sergeant Snow was seriously wounded on the opening day of the attack on the infamous and formidable Hindenburg Line at Ronssoy in France, which commenced on 18 September 1918. As a result of shrapnel wounds to his back, chest and abdomen he was returned to England and remained hospitalised until 20 December 1918 when he was discharged from the Army.

A constant reminder of his wounds, received in battle, was a jagged piece of shrapnel which had lodged between his heart and one of his lungs. Over the years Arthur Snow visited hospitals in various parts of the country in the hope that surgery could effect its reward. Finally, in 1965, he coughed up the piece of shrapnel which had threatened his life for 47 years. The manner of the releasing of the unwanted obstruction was described by doctors as 'a medical miracle'.

We had a 1½ armed window cleaner, Dizza Boulter, who hooked his short ladder over his half arm and cycled around Wigston cleaning windows.

The tale told by soldier Mason, a war veteran who joined the regular peacetime army after 1919. He told of a sergeant-major found dead sitting on the latrine. In the midst of battle two detectives came from Scotland Yard to investigate the death. The shot angle could not have been a German one. No one was charged as most had been killed. Soldier Mason did add that the man was 'an evil sod' and deserved it.

The evidence of the terrible loss of life was apparent when I asked why Annie Orton of Harcourt Road, even in old age a pretty, pleasant woman, never married and mother replied 'There were so few men came home to marry'.

Proud Brothers in Arms. Seated are Sergeant Arthur Snow and Company Sergeant-Major Edward Snow. Standing is Private Alfred Snow. (Don Snow)

The aftermath reached way into time. Mr Robinson, the Wigston gravedigger, lived on Bull Head Street, Candlelight Row to be precise. Each side of his fireplace stood a highly polished shell. On his son's death I enquired about them and learned panic had occurred when it was discovered that they were 'live'. So Bull Head Street could have disappeared one night when an extra fire had been lit.

Curtis Weston of South Wigston as a Boy Scout was sent to France as a messenger. He was seconded to The Seaforth Highlanders. Bikes were issued as sore buttocks occurred because kilts were of course material and so a special dispensation was granted to wear pants. His kilt, badges and Glengarry are now at Snibston Museum in Leicestershire.

Private Curtis Weston, The Seaforth Highlanders. (Duncan Lucas)

My father told of the Aussie troops being welcomed as they would not accept the vicious field punishment, e.g. tied spread-eagled to a field gun wheel whilst it was being fired. The Aussies cut them down and the British officers dared not stop them.

The village almost enlisting en masse – Two Steeples' lads an example but the cruelty of some women, who gave out white feathers to men not in uniform whom they considered cowards, some were wounded or men on leave!

'Deafy' Cottam, stone deaf, he was blown up in Russia after 1918 whilst the British force was fighting with the White Russians.

Bernard Bent, who travelled around with a threshing drum, told how he was in a machine-gun crew. It was so lethal that it was moved from site to site rapidly as the Germans shelled it; so as it left a position the poor troops left behind knew a bombardment was coming. The old soldiers in the threshing teams told Bernard their modest thoughts.

8

THE FIRST WORLD WAR
BY DUNCAN LUCAS
AS TOLD BY PRIVATE ORSON LUCAS

Transcribed by Emily Lucas, great-granddaughter to Orson Lucas. Emily and Orson never met, Emily being born some years after Orson passed away, but she has been able to relate to him via the work she has undertaken here. She has also come to a great appreciation of the First World War and its impact on ordinary people due to this.

The transcript is of Orson (O) talking to his son Brian (B) whilst looking at battlefield maps.

O: I arrived after the first day of the Somme and we were pushed up. It wasn't a disorderly retreat as everybody thinks it was but we didn't know where the hell we were. We went to Noyon and we got round near Roye somewhere then we cut across to Nel to try and force them off again but they beat us and eventually we retired somewhere right up to here, near just in front of Amiens, and when we got there we knew damn well we wouldn't get any further. Although we were, I'd got one footy on, just me gas mask. I'd lost every pack, I'd got a handle here of …

B: Ammunition?

O: Ammunition, and me rifle and bayonet. And when we got somewhere near there, we got on a road. And the artillery, we couldn't move along the road. Our artillery had got the positions on the road. We hadn't fired or done sweet nothing. We knew damn well we weren't gonna get far then. And when we got there they sort of called us all out, made a company of all of us. There were Manchesters, Leicesters, Royal Skins, Scots and Drops and everything. And they formed us all into one company and we were going to attack. But what happened we don't know. We were never called on. Then we were sorted out, the Manchesters. We were sent somewhere up here on the coast for a holiday.

We had been in, I don't know how long we had been in there and they sent us up here somewhere for a holiday. We were going to be at least three weeks. We were broken up, the battalion, well it wasn't a battalion. It wasn't a boys brigade. It was cut up to nothing. Anyway, we got up to this place and ooh it was grand here, in the sea it was beautiful. We lay back and the next day he said calling, we're off for Liverpool, we're gonna need you. Right, bang. Off we went. The Germans had broken through.

Near Ypres.

They'd broken through down here. The whole time, the whole war, they never took Ypres. They wanted to take that. If they'd have took that it would've meant?

B: They could have got through to the Channel Ports.

O: But they never did take it and we own it. The British owned it the whole of the war. There's a canal somewhere there. And we were at a place called Spoil Bank on the canal. And I was in charge of a Lewis gun then at the time. Not a machine gun. You couldn't traverse with them. I mean if you wanted to traverse with them you had to hold onto your shoulder like that. It was point blank. But I was in charge of the Lewis gun and I was sent to hold a place on our flank. And it was a lovely spot. We got into a nice little bungalow, it was really great and it were beautiful. And then we were chased out of that and I retired right back to the battalion there. Somewhere near Ypres.

On Spoil Bank again. Well, then they broke through on the right and I was the only one that knew where the stand to take position was for the Lewis gun. I was in charge of it you see. And I, er, I was taking this Lewis gun section up and we got so fed up walking in the blinking trenches that we were walking on the top. And I said, Oh Christ I've lost my way, I don't know where it is. And I said ooh here it is look, just on the right. Just as I turned round like that, 'Bang!'

I got a sniper. Quarter-past. There was a sniper. I'd just spotted where we'd got to go and just as I turned round, he let fire. And he hit me there. He took the bottom off me left pocket, went through all the contents, we all carried a wallet full of photographs in that pocket. It made a hole there. Cut underneath, through the breastbone. Not underneath it, through 2 ribs and never touched a bone and come out this side and went through the wallet here.

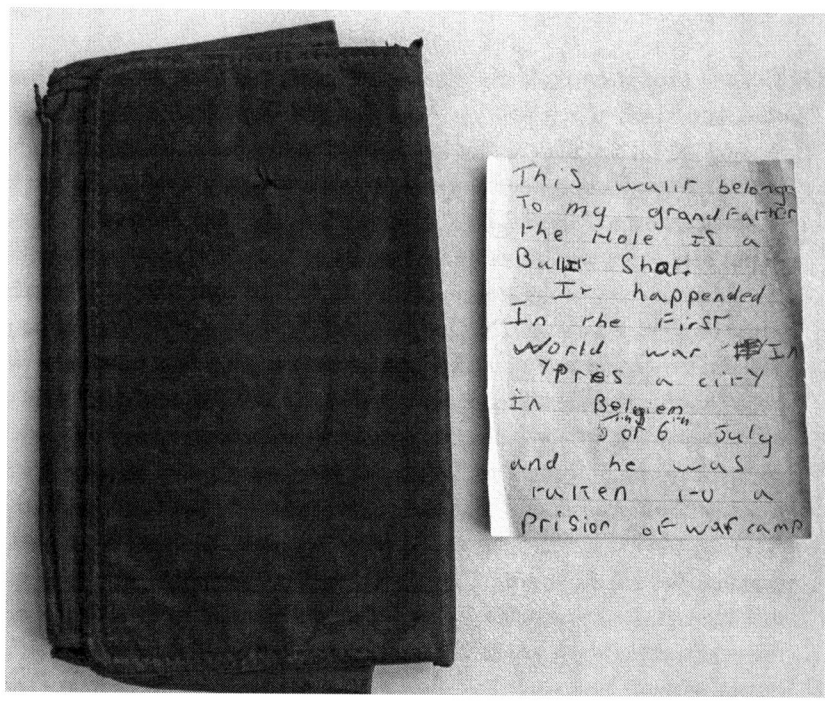

This walit belongs
To my grandfather
the Hole is a
Bullet Shot.
  It happended
In the First
World war In
Ypres a city
In Belgien
        5 or 6" July
and he was
ra[[en i-o a
Prision of war camp

Private Orson Lucas' wallet. (Duncan Lucas)

Three of the pictures through which the bullet passed. (Duncan Lucas)

B: I remember seeing the wallet. We used to have it at home, we used to play with it.

O: Oh and they always told me, these blokes that had been wounded, they said, you know when you get wounded you don't realise you've been wounded. You don't feel it. But my God when that bullet hit me I thought it was a horse kicking me. I turned two somersaults and fell in the ditch, in the trench and I lay out there, honestly thought I was finished.

But I lay out there, I don't know how many hours and eventually, one of my old sergeants saw me and he was a toff. And he says, what's the matter with you then, what's up? Oh God he says, I'll get the stretcher up for you. You can't walk and I couldn't. He says let me put a bandage round and he put a bandage round and made me comfortable and says now don't worry, we'll get you in. Not long after, the stretcher bearers came up and they took me back to the dressing area. It was the first time I'd seen an American. It was an American doctor that had come up. And he was in a big tunnel, and they carried me in there. And I saw this doctor, he dressed me, good dressing. And I said I've got off lightly doc and he says yeah, no doubt about that. He says, don't worry, we've sent for the ambulances. He says, they're on the road and we've got several in here all going in the ambulances and you'll be one of them. Says, you'll be home, he says, in about two days. Thank God for that. And all at once, on this tunnel there's one of our blokes at the end on guard with the Lewis gun and I could see him at the end of the tunnel and all at once he's picked his gun up and da da da da da and the Germans are on the top of the tunnel, on the top of the dugout. I thought my God, what's up here? And what had happened is the Frenchmen had chucked their hands up on Mount Kemmel.

B: Yeah.

O: Retired and the Germans had come round them. And I was taken prisoner in that dressing room. About twenty-four hours before they took the front line. You know what it was, our men were holding out on the front line.

B: And they'd come all out through the back.

O: And the Jerries come up and my gas mask had gone, they pinched that. They'd taken me shoes off. Those men had to make you comfortable in the dressing station. And I lay on a stretcher and thought, my God, I'm not gonna stand this and this bloke, if ever a bloke deserved a medal, he did. He stood there firing, keeping them away. Eventually, fell dead. And the Jerries started to fire through this tunnel. It were a long tunnel. I thought I'm not getting away from this. And I rolled off this stretcher and every so far there was a tiny alcove you know, where you could crawl in.

B: Yeah.

O: It was a masterpiece of dugouts.

B: Yeah.

O: And I crawled out the way, they could fire up the tunnel and missed me but eventually they come and got us, the Jerries did. They carried me outside and then it was the Jerries stood there, and all at once our people started firing gas shells. They knew that the Jerries had taken us but they started firing gas shells at the Jerries. And oh my God, you could hear 'em. They dropped, you could tell a gas shell, it used to drop (makes click sound with mouth), just like a dove. And all at once you'd feel the gas come. I wonder if that was anything to do with this. You didn't get much of it. It put the wind up the Jerries. They didn't like it although they started the gas strike. They got us all together somehow, I don't know and they said the only way I could get down, they didn't bother about the wounded, was if my own men would carry me down on the stretcher. I couldn't walk. They was four or five of my own men that volunteered to carry me … They tipped me off the stretcher, couldn't help it, I mean we were going over rough ground. Eventually they got me to somewhere. Ooh now let me see if I can find it on this map. I doubt it. Ah, we got somewhere out there. I'm not quite sure the place where. It'd be that road, which would be this side of Ypres, somewhere near there. But anyway, they carried me so far then bunged me in a dugout er, pill box and I was left there. And I thought, what's going to happen now? They took all the other prisoners away that could walk. The Germans then said well if a man is wounded, then that is his punishment. But if you're hearty and strong and there's nothing wrong with you, you know, then they take you to work behind the line. But eventually somehow, what happened I don't know, they put me in an old van. We went sailing off jumpin' and bumpin', and they dropped me in some church for one night and we had a cup of coffee, their coffee – made of acorns. It was terrible stuff. And nothing else.

Then we went on from there and there we were in a convent for a day or two. We still couldn't walk but they did do their best to dress us. But what they did was this: we'd all got bandages on. You know how the army bandage you up. In special things on here, on my two wounds. And I can remember now a doctor saying oh, too good for you. These can be used for the Fatherland. And he took all my dressings off, sent 'em, put 'em in the laundry basket and gonna wash them and use them for the Germans. And then they got mine and put some kind of a coating or something on it. And their cotton, I'm talking Irish here, their cotton wool was all paper. I mean it was nice, it was nice how they did it. They put some of that on this little piece of er, what do we call it?

B: Gauze?

O: Gauze. Then they cut a piece of paper, thick paper, white paper. Good stuff mind you. Then they painted something round it like that then they put it over and stuck it on and the same that side. So I got two like that sticking out instead of how we put bandages all around, they hadn't got 'em. I had them there. They said, that'll do for you. We were sent from there to that place.

B: Ghent?

O: Ghent, yes or Gon we used to call it. Well there, I was feeling better from the damage and I started to walk. And I'd had a wrist watch sent to me from home and it was a black dial and it wouldn't go and (laughs) I'd got a beard at that time. And while I was there, there was a posh sergeant, a German sergeant and he says to me, speaking English, do you want to sell that watch? I says you can have it. He says, well how much do you want for it? I say five francs. He goes, what's a franc? I says well, five marks then. He says, right it looks good. So he took it off and give me five marks. I got that and of course we were all part for sharing so we all said well let's go and see if we can get a shave. We walked down into the courtyard and there was a barber there, a German barber. And er, we asked him if he'd shave us. And we were all scared stiff in case he slit our throats but he said yes. And he charged us a ha'penny. In those days, a ha'penny, the value was probably about half a mark or half a penny or something. And they'd got no real soap. Well, what we got really was a sort of pumice stone and he just wet it and rubbed it round me beard and he got a razor and sharpened it up and he went down and went right round it like that, once. And it was the best shave I've ever had in my life. And we gave him the money, there were about seven of us I think and we went back to where we were all lying down in this prisoner of war place waiting for transportation to a camp and one of my pals comes up and says hey, for God's sake get out of it. He says, that Jerry's comin' round that you sold that watch to. He says, he'll bloody murder you. He said the watch won't go. I said, I know it won't but I wasn't going to tell him that. He offered us five marks and we wanted it to get what we could. And I could see him at the top looking at everyone. And they hid me behind some er, bits of kit that they'd got. And I was shaking as he came round and they said, ah he's gone away, he's gone with the other lot now to some camp. (Impersonates German sergeant) 'Urr that bugger camp, my money.'

Anyway I was lucky because the same day, we all had to, they packed us into a carriage. I will say this; it was a proper carriage, better than the French. We travelled in France in horse boxes and we left there, Ghent, and we eventually found ourselves, ooh over here and down here, Frankfurt on the Maine now where's that?

B: Over here somewhere.

O: We went through Cologne.

B: It's probably over here, further on. It's not on the map, probably.

O: We went to Frankfurt on the Maine. A place called Giessen. And we stopped at one or two stations on the road and er, on our train there want many of us on it, but on our train was a lot of German wounded going back and at these particular stations where they stop, the nurses, there, the Germany nurses, were handing out drinks and everything and cigarettes to the er to the German wounded and we asked them if we could but they wouldn't give a damn thing. We never had a damn thing at all. Eventually we got to Giessen.

It was on Frankfurt on the Maine and we all marched, what was left of us, to this barracks. And there was a lazarette at the hospital and I was bunged straight in there. We walked across there in no shoes, and I'd got me old tunic on with all bloodstains all down the front, still got that on. No shoes at all. And a Jerry, a private, er not a private, a civilian took pity on two of us and they daren't give us 'em. They chucked 'em out to us, a pair of old shoes. I'd got oddens but they fitted. And I walked 'bout with those until the end of the blinkin' war. Oh no, I got some out in a parcel from home. That was it. And I was bunged in hospital and I thought blimey, it was beautiful. And we always had, one night a week, we had what I called and everybody thought was a posh meal. We had that Dutch cheese with the holes in it.

We had a bit of that and well they call it black bread but it wasn't black it was brown. I didn't object to it at all but it want like being at home. And er, on this particular day, I'd been in hospital about a fortnight. There was a doctor would come and examine you and give you injections, and there was a sergeant, a French sergeant that would interpret and tell them all. And on this particular day he says get ready, you're for the camp. I thought oh my God, it's the day I don't want to go because that was the day we had the cheese. But I had to go across into the camp. And it wasn't far, just across the road. And er, when we got there I says, oh my God was goin' on, we're got nothing. We'd got nothing. And all they gave us was this sauerkraut. And it stunk. Ooh it was hell. The real sauerkraut, I believe they tell me, is very good.

B: It is.

O: But my God, this stuff, ooh it stank awful. And erm, I happened to drop across some Canadians. And they were real good sorts. And they said to me, aren't you getting any parcels through? And I says, no. They says, how long have you been a prisoner then? So I told them. They says, have you been on check roll call? I says, what's that? They said, God blimey, they don't known you're here you lucky B_____. They says, look, tell you what we'll do. Ten of them, says, you can join our mess, 'cause the prisoners then, they had their parcels sent. They were getting parcels from the British Red Cross. They put all the parcels together and formed a kind of mess. They said, look after us and do the cooking for us … do the cooking? I said, it's all tinned stuff. They said, look after us and do the washing up and we'll find you the food. God, they thought it was gorgeous. Now they said, they don't know you're here. We've had a check roll call and your name weren't called out. Now they said, look, when we go out, we had to go out every day, they says, when your name's called, for the check roll call, he says, when there's a check roll call we'll give you the tip, stand between us. And we did. And the check roll call, that meant that everyman had to answer his name. And as he answered his name he walked away.

B: Yeah.

O: And he says, we'll cover you. And (laughing) you know what they did? They passed word down the line and you could see it was a check roll call because they got them calling. And I stood between two Canadians and there was two more each side and when their names was called, they'd go ooh, gosh I'm starving. They were just hanging around you see. And then when there were two or three of them, I went and joined with 'em you see. And they hadn't got sense enough to see that I'd gone with 'em and as soon as I joined up with this three or four, we went back in.

B: Yeah.

O: And I was never traced, oh, for a hell of a time. And eventually they did find me and I was sent to work in an iron foundry at Offenbach I think they called it. I'll never forget the name of the firm I worked for. It was er, a big old company. Lavissohn. L-A-V-I-S-S-O-H-N. That's how it was spelt.

And we got there and there was only one other Englishman on this commando. They called them commandos. There were, oh, thousands attached to this camp at Giessen. And I mean if they'd all have been there, they'd never have held 'em. Some had gone to salt mines, some had gone to farms and to factories, all over. But all of your mail went through Giessen, the head camp you see. You were attached to that camp. And he took about, and I sent him one. He was an old possum, we called him a possum. He was a, er a Prussian guard and had contracted chronic rheumatism on the Eastern front and he was in charge of us and he turned out to be a damn good sort. He was posted. Where we went, he dropped me first of all, where we were going to live. And, in this hut, well it wasn't a hut: it was like an odd stop in a shop. And the old possum had got a part took off and he looked after us and he'd got his bed in that side. And there was, er, four Frenchmen, four Russians, two Englishmen and an Italian, all in this place together. And no one could understand each other, only bits and pieces. And this fellow, he belonged to the King's Own that was a prisoner of war there. Well, after I'd done what bit of stuff I'd got, it weren't much, he took us up to the factory, the guard did. And when I walked up to that factory, that iron foundry, this bloke he nearly, he says 'Ooh God,' he says, 'an Englishman.' Ooh, he says, thank God, he says, I've been waiting for a pal. He says, I haven't got a bloody pal here at all. He says, you're going back anyway. He says, have you got a part. I says, good God no, I've only been took prisoner not many weeks. He says, well look, he says, he told me, that locker I've got there, he says, when you get back open it and he says, you'll find all my parcels in there. He says, there's plenty of Woodbines, help yourself. That's the spirit that was about then. You don't get it now do you?

And he took me back and it was late in the day then. They didn't finish work until about six o'clock at night. I went back and I had a cigarette and ooh it were lovely. I hadn't had one for ooh, months and months and months. And er, they came back and we made a … He says, don't worry, he says, I'll share all we got. And I says, well I've got nothing to share. And he says, well don't worry, you'll get your parcels through. And eventually I got 'em through, but the next day I was taken to work at this er …

B: Foundry?

O: Foundry. And er, said as well as he could, bloody foreman. The foreman had got an office there so he could see if everybody were working or not. And didn't they treat 'em rough. But I wasn't treated bad at all compared to some of them. And as soon as I got there they were, 'You come on this.' I'd never seen one before. They put me on a machine. They thought because I was British, I knew everything. And what it was, the girders had come through on the machine, it was a punch. And there was an old fellow who understood the work, he was an engineer. And he was measuring and having a punch hole.

B: Yeah.

O: So he shows where they got to be. And then they'd come through on a roller to go through this machine and he told me, he says, when they get to a certain spot, when they line up with that punch hole with that, pull that lever and it will punch a hole right through it. And it'll go back itself automatically and another will come through. He says, it's easy, you'll manage it. I says, okay (laughs). I tried to work it. First time I pulled it, it come up in the wrong place. Smashed the machine all about. And I didn't do it on purpose, they said I had. Well I got two days' cells for that. One cell and two days on me own with nothing to eat, but this bloke looked after me and we'd got a German there who was a real toff. He told me when the war had finished. But this Englishman, when he comes to me he says, if they ask you what you can do, tell 'em you're a painter. He says, there's a hell of lot of painting wants doing here. It's just easy. They used 'em for concrete like grids you know. And there was hundreds of 'em made. And I got my job painting these round. So he says to me, what can you do? So I says, well I'm a painter by trade. Ah, just what we want, and they gave me the simplest job possible. So I'm painting and painting and helping this Jerry who was a toff and told me how to go on all the lot. And at the finish he says … oh, we went into the yard where all the bits of steel and everything was and this fellow showing me all the bits. I says, what's all that about? And this was late on about November time. He says, oh there's a meeting here, he says, they're going mad, he says, we're in a hell of a mess, we're beaten. We used to have a paper circulated to prisoners of war called the *Continental Times*. Mind you, it was all against things, trying to turn us and all the rest. But one of us spotted, he says, hey, it said in this paper, and I read it, that General Haig had been seen in Ostend. I said Ostend? God's truth, I said, where the hell have they advanced? I said, they must be advancing fast then. That was the first we knew. And it was in Ostend and when I was taken prisoner of war it was down here.

So you can tell that they was coming this way and pushed 'em back. But anyway, towards the end of it there was this big meeting in the town of Offenbach. And this bloke told me, he says, the guys are going to abdicate. Never heard anymore until November the 11th or 12th and this guy says

Carl Voltgartner and family, Offenbach, with whom Private Lucas was billeted whilst at Geissen POW Camp in May 1918. (Duncan Lucas)

to me, you'll want to get out, quick. Go and see the boss he says. The war is finished. Nah, I said, get out of it. He says, it's finished. The Armistice is signed. It was signed yesterday at eleven o'clock. As best he could in English he says, and they've got you so much and all prisoners must be released. He says, and don't tell 'em I've told you for God's sake (coughs). So I went to the boss and told him. I said the war's finished, let me go back to camp.

9

THE POPPY AND THE SHAMROCK
BY DUNCAN LUCAS

LESLIE HEDGES FORRYAN

Leslie Hedges Forryan, or Les as he was known, was born in Bell Street, Great Wigston, in 1891. He was one of six brothers, four of whom went to war in 1914. One, Arnold, was gassed and suffered the rest of his long life farming in Newgate End. Herbert was wounded by a shell blast and found near death in a shell crater; he lost an eye. He became a grocer at West Bridgford, Nottingham. Finally, there was Percy who served in the 'mechanised' Army Service Corps (ASC) and returned safely to Great Wigston after the war.

Les, who survived unscathed, joined up with his friend Johnson who went into the Leicestershire Yeomanry and was killed. Les went to war in the Army Service Corps (ASC) to serve with his

Private Leslie Hedges Forryan with 'a friend'. (Duncan Lucas)

beloved heavy horses. He told of the mud that swallowed horse and cart, of the carnage and the affection twixt man and horse.

He loved flowers, as is obvious from the pressed poppy from Flanders that he carried in his testament. This testament, dated 1915, was in Duncan Lucas' archives, and as Captain Benjamin Daetwyler (Australian Army) had Duncan's father's medals and badges, he felt Benjamin would be a good custodian of it.

Prior to packing, Ben's grandfather, Max Daetwyler, Duncan's brother-in-law, discovered a pressed poppy in it and further on a pressed shamrock. As the testament was in Les Forryan's name and he had been in Flanders and also Dublin

Leslie Hedges Forryan with Maggie May Boulter on their wedding day in 1919. (Duncan Lucas)

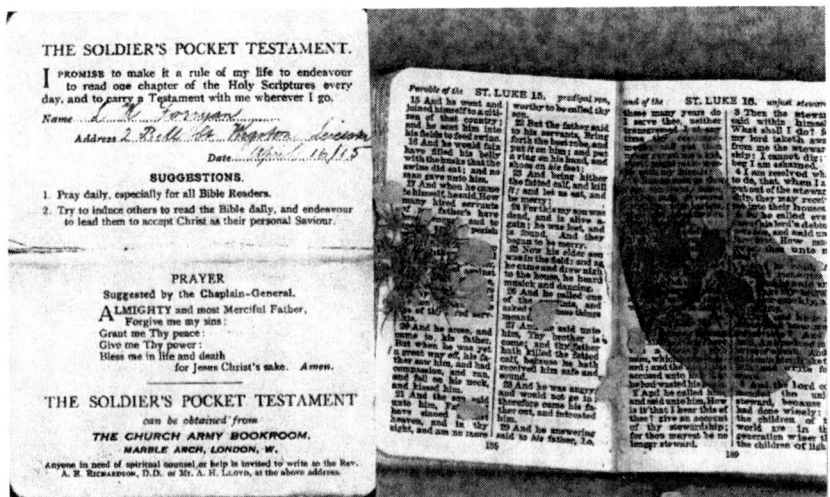

Private Forryan's Pocket Testament containing the pressed Poppy and the Shamrock. (Duncan Lucas)

in 1916, it was obvious that here was a very rare original item indeed. The Poppy Shamrock Testament with photos is now on display at the United Reformed Church, Long Street, Wigston Magna.

When working in the fields in peacetime he told of deeper ploughing bringing up long dormant seeds and the evidence of that with the red mass of Flanders poppies. To confirm his views the Shamrock also enclosed in the testament bears witness to his journey to Dublin in 1916 during the uprising. He told of instructions to keep on the wagons whilst in Dublin otherwise the women will 'lynch you'. Outside Dublin, where obviously the shamrock came from, he said the Irish were lovely.

Les was proud of his family and his native village. His Hedges 'Christian' name was his mother's maiden name – she came from Wytham, Oxfordshire. Hence he was known as Leslie Hedges Forryan. He married Maggie Mary Boulter in 1919 at the Independent Chapel in Wigston Magna.

There was also his pride in his forebears, one of whom fought at Waterloo. John Forryan, Armourer Sergeant 3rd Battalion, The Grenadier Guards, 1810–1851 served forty-three years and five months, part of which was in the Peninsular War (1811–1814) and at Waterloo.

This is a story of a man who fought for King and Country. This man, Les Forryan, a true countryman, preserved living proof of that with a simple Poppy and Shamrock.

Second Lieutenant Donald Forryan, The King's Shropshire Light Infantry, attached to The King's Own Yorkshire Light Infantry, killed in action at the Battle of the Somme 16 September 1916. He was the second son of John George and Elizabeth Forryan. (Duncan Lucas)

In contrast, this Forryan family fared well during the war with all brothers returning safely to their home village, whilst three of the four sons of John George Forryan of Great Wigston were all killed in action, never to return to their beloved country.

10

HOME TO REST

BY TRICIA BERRY

The Commonwealth War Graves Commission's records for the First World War list eleven military burials at Wigston Cemetery. All but one are marked with the familiar official white headstone and all are situated to the south of the chapel in sections B, C and D. Any soldier who died even as late as 1920 received an official burial if their death was judged to have been due to their military service. Only soldiers who served overseas were eligible to receive war medals. This chapter has been researched and written in memory of all the local men who lost their lives, or suffered damage to their health, in this dreadful conflict. These eleven, tragic though their stories are, at least could be buried where they wished, in familiar surroundings close to home.

Private Walter Harrison, 4th Battalion, The Leicestershire Regiment, No: 5041. Died 19 December 1915, aged 28.
Walter was born in Wigston around 1887, the son of George Harrison, a shopkeeper/framework knitter, and his wife Ann. Both his parents were also Wigston born. In 1911 the family lived at No. 63 Long Street. Walter worked as a Post Office boy, then in the family business as a salt hawker. On 6 July 1912 he married Annie Corbett at Blaby District Register Office, giving his occupation as a journeyman carriage builder. Annie was the daughter of John Corbett a farmworker of No. 10 Newton Lane. The couple set up home at No. 77 Long Street and had two sons, Walter and Douglas.

On 28 June 1915, at Leicester, he joined the Territorial Force of The Leicestershire Regiment for four years' service. Just over four months later, on 5 November, while stationed at Belton Park, near Grantham, he was discharged as medically unfit. Belton is now a National Trust Property, but at this time was the home of Earl Brownlow, who had put it at the disposal of the War Office for training purposes. Walter was admitted on a Military Order to the Leicestershire & Rutland Asylum at Narborough suffering from melancholia. On 19 December he was reported missing, and his body was later discovered on the London/North Western Railway Line in Cosby parish. The coroner's inquest was held by Mr G. Bouskell, who stated: 'There is no conclusive evidence to support an assumption [of suicide],' and returned a verdict that 'the deceased was run over by a train, and that no blame is attributable to anyone'.

Colour-Sergeant William John Gurr, 3rd Battalion, The Leicestershire Regiment, No: 12902. Died 6 July 1916, aged 43.

William was born on 28 July 1872 at No. 46 Blisset Street, Southwark, Surrey (in the ancient parish of St Olave). He was the son of Silas Gurr, a greengrocer/police sergeant, and his wife Selina, who were natives of Surrey and Kent respectively. When both parents tragically died in 1879, William and his siblings, Emily and Albert, became pupils at the South Metropolitan District Boarding School in Sutton, Surrey.

On 4 October 1886, William signed a Long Service Attestation (twelve years) at Aldershot with The Leicestershire Regiment. He was only 14 years old, 4ft 6ins tall and his calling or trade was listed as musician – a skill which was probably why he was accepted so young. Army life suited him well and over time he twice requested extensions to his length of service. He was posted to Bermuda, Halifax (Nova Scotia), West Indies, South Africa (twice), Egypt and India as well as periods of home (in the UK) duty. He was promoted to Corporal in 1895 and Colour-Sergeant in 1898 and received the Queen's South African Medal (Transvaal) 1902 award for service in the Boer War. He was upgraded to first-class service pay and his conduct is recorded as exemplary. Not many attained such a high level.

He applied for discharge and left the service in 1910, by which time he was 38 years old and living at No. 17 Midland Cottages, South Wigston. He obtained a job at Two Steeples Ltd. as a hosiery stock-keeper, and on 12 October 1912 at Blaby District Register Office he married Dorothy May Clare, twenty years his junior. Dorothy worked as a shoe machinist and lived at No. 49 Blaby Road, her father was Benjamin Castledine Clare, a journeyman painter. The couple set up home at No. 24 Bassett Street and had two daughters, Irene and Dorothy.

Following the outbreak of war, William enlisted again on 29 August 1914 at Leicester into his old regiment for one year's service with the Army Reserve (Special Reservists). It is reported in *The Leicester Daily Mercury* of 3 September 1914 that: 'A party of 16 recruits from Two Steeples under the

The grave of Colour-Sergeant William John Gurr in Wigston Cemetery. (Tricia Berry)

War wedding was the theme of this clever entry in a fancy dress procession held in South Wigston in 1915/16, to raise money for parcels for the troops. The groom wears military uniform complete with two medals and three chevrons on his right arm, and two of the guests are wounded soldiers. (Tricia Berry)

command of Colour-Sergeant Gurr ... have left the barracks [at Glen Parva]. They met with a great reception, the female employees accompanying them en masse, many carrying flags. They were played to the station by Mr Charles Moore's Band.'

On 26 June 1916 he was admitted to the 5th Northern General Hospital (now the administration block of the University of Leicester) suffering from gastric dilatation due to ulcers. He died the following month from this, and from shock following an operation to try and relieve it.

In 1920 his widow Dorothy remarried and became Mrs Edward P. Cosgrave.

Private Ernest William Seaton, 6th (Service) Battalion, The Leicestershire Regiment, No: 10925. Died 23 September 1916, aged 24.

Ernest was born at Wigston in 1892, the son of Samuel Seaton a bricklayer and his wife Ann, who were both also Wigston born. In 1911 the family lived at No. 86 Leicester Road. He was employed in the boot trade but was working as a bricklayer when he joined The Leicestershire Regiment, signing up in Leicester on 1 September 1914 for the duration of the war. Dr Arthur Nathaniel Barnley, a Wigston doctor who lived at Kingswood Lodge, Bushloe End, was present and performed the required medical examination.

On 29 July 1915 Ernest was posted to France. During a brief period of leave he married Lilian Grace Read at Knighton Church on 21 June 1916, by licence. Lilian was a hosiery hand, and daughter of Walter Read, a bricklayer's labourer. The couple lived at her family home at No. 75 Montague Road, Clarendon Park, Leicester.

On 15 July 1916 he suffered a gunshot wound to the head and injury to his hand and was moved to hospital in Rouen. He was reported to be seriously ill, though improving, but on 2 September he was returned to the United Kingdom and admitted to the 1st Southern General Hospital, Birmingham, where he died three weeks later. He had a son, also named Ernest, who was born posthumously.

He was awarded the 1914/15 Star and British War and Victory Medals.

Private William Hopkins, The King's Own (Royal Lancaster Regiment), No: 5605. Died 12 July 1918, aged 42.

William was born at Wigston in 1876, the son of George, an agricultural labourer from Glen Parva, and his wife Jane, born in Wigston. He worked as a shoe riveter and lived at home with his family in Victoria Street. On 24 January 1896 at Leicester he joined The King's Own Scottish Borderers, agreeing to serve for twelve years, seven with the Colours and five in the Reserve. In the event he served eight years, one year at home and seven in the East Indies, being awarded the Indian 1895 Medal with clasps for service on the Punjab Frontier 1897–9 and Tirah Expeditionary Force 1897–8. He was transferred to the Army Reserve in 1904 and returned to the shoe trade before being discharged on 23 January 1908.

On 10 November 1906 at Blaby District Register Office he married Nellie Hutchinson, a shoe hand who lived in North Street. In 1911 the couple were living at No. 22 Mowsley End and had a son, George, and two daughters, Lilian and Ethel. Subsequently four further children, Annie, Charles, Mabel and William, were to be born, the latter posthumously.

On 11 December 1915, by then aged 39, he enlisted again, this time at Glen Parva, into The Leicestershire Regiment for the duration of the war with the Colours and in the Army Reserve. Initially in the Reserve, he was mobilised on 24 August 1916 and after four months training embarked to join the British Expeditionary Force on 22 December 1916. The following day he was transferred to The King's Own (Royal Lancaster Regiment). He was seriously wounded on 2 April 1917 and admitted to hospital, then transferred to the United Kingdom twenty-three days later. On 12 October he was discharged from the army, being no longer fit for war service. He died at home in Mowsley End on 12 July 1918 as a result of the injury he had received.

He was awarded the British War and Victory Medals.

Commemorated on his gravestone is Private William Hopkins, his son, who was killed in Malaya on 10 December 1941, aged 23.

A military funeral procession in South Wigston, 1915. Note all the soldiers are carrying their rifles in the dipped position. Leading the bearer party is Sergeant Ernest Oscar Powdrill of Fleckney, who survived the war to return to his teaching post at South Wigston Boys' School. The gentleman behind him wearing a bowler hat is believed to be Councillor John Wycliffe Black JP. (Tricia Berry)

Company Sergeant-Major George Walter Goodman, 53rd (YS) Training Battalion, The Northumberland Fusiliers, No:TR5/1950. Died 20 November 1918, aged 34.

George was born in Leicester in 1884, the son of Walter Goodman, a shoe riveter, born in Wellingborough and his wife Jane, born in nearby Wilby. The family lived at No. 36 New Park Street, Leicester, but by 1911 had moved to Marstown Avenue, Glen Parva. George also worked as a shoe riveter. On 3 June 1911 he married Grace Evelyn Florence Caroline Holland at St Thomas' Church, South Wigston. Grace was the daughter of Thomas Holland, a newsagent, and the family lived in Kirkdale Road, South Wigston. The couple set up home at 59 Clifford Street and had two daughters, Florence and Evelyn.

On 3 September 1914 he enlisted at Glen Parva, into the 8th (Service) Battalion, The Leicestershire Regiment, for the duration of the war. He was sent for training at Rugeley and was plainly a very capable soldier, being promoted Lance-Corporal on 15 October, Corporal on 15 November, and Sergeant on 15 December. On 29 July 1915 he embarked to join the Expeditionary Force in France. By 6 September 1915 he had been returned to the United Kingdom injured. In May 1917 he was transferred to the 5th Training Battalion of his Regiment, before being transferred again on 3 July 1917 to the 53rd (YS) Battalion Training Regiment of The Northumberland Fusiliers.

Wigston Temperance Silver Prize Band proudly displaying their trophies in the garden of
The Elms, Bushloe End. On the front row: left of the trophy table is Charles Moore (band leader),
on the right of it J.D. Broughton (president) and next to him J.G. Hurst (secretary). The band was
much in demand during this time, leading troops from barracks to railway station, playing for
fundraising events and afterwards for Peace Celebrations and Memorial Events. (Tricia Berry)

He was taken ill with the notorious influenza, which turned into septic
pneumonia and had been hospitalised for twenty-eight days when he died
on 20 November 1918 at the Military Hospital, Clipstone, near to Southwell,
Nottinghamshire.

He was awarded the 1914/15 Star and British War and Victory Medals.

Gunner Edwin Noble, The Royal Garrison Artillery, No: 198252. Died 22 November 1918, aged 37.

Edwin was born in Wigston in 1881, the son of Henry Noble, a framework
knitter, and his wife Eliza, who were both also Wigston born. In 1911 the
family lived at No. 5 Welford Road. He worked as a hosiery hand and
later, like his father, became a framework knitter. On 9 December 1915 at
Leicester he signed up with The Royal Regiment of Artillery for the duration
of the war, and was put on Army Reserve. On 27 January 1917, no doubt
aware of his imminent call-up, he married Rachel Ellen Coxall, by licence
at All Saints' Church, Wigston. Rachel was the daughter of Alfred Coxall,
a baker, and the family lived at Avenue House, No. 1 Central Avenue (now a
veterinary surgery), where Edwin and Rachel also lived after their marriage.

On 2 February 1917 he was mobilised and reported at Newcastle to join
The Royal Field Artillery. Only sixteen days later he was admitted to the

A mass-produced postcard for brief messages to those overseas. The word postcard is printed on the reverse in sixteen different languages. (Tricia Berry)

Military Hospital, Cork, Ireland, then transferred for further treatment to Queenstown. He had influenza, which later developed into pleurisy and bronchitis and he was also found to be anaemic. He recovered and on 29 July was transferred to The Royal Garrison Artillery (heavy larger-calibre guns) on coastal protection duties. The following winter he again developed influenza, which rapidly turned into pneumonia. He died within five days, on 22 November 1918, at the Victoria Street Hall, Kirkwall, Orkney in Scotland.

Edwin's burial is the one without a military headstone because his widow decided to purchase the plot.

Corporal George Ernest Preston, 28th Battalion, The Durham Light Infantry, No: 75123. Died 17 December 1918, aged 27.

George was born 24 February 1891 in North Street, Wigston, the son of William, a sock framework knitter born in Wigston, and his wife Jane, born in Blaby. In 1911 the family lived in Oadby Lane. He worked as a shoe cutter and later as a house painter. On 8 September 1914 he signed up in Leicester with The Leicestershire Regiment for the duration of the war. He spent the first year on home duties, before departing to join the Expeditionary Force in France on 29 July 1915. He was promoted Lance-Corporal on 25 May 1916 and then Corporal on 25 September 1916. He spent short spells in hospital with tonsillitis and then with a carbuncle on his neck before being transferred to the United Kingdom on 20 February 1917.

On 17 May 1917 he married, by licence at All Saints' Church, Ethel Egley (née Revell), who, although only 19 years old, was already a widow. She was the daughter of Abraham Revell, a collier. The couple made their home at her address: No. 22 North Street. During the remainder of the war he was posted to four different regiments: 9th Battalion, The Royal Defence Corps, 3rd Battalion, The King's Own Yorkshire Light Infantry, 14th Battalion, The Duke of Wellington's (West Riding Regiment) and 28th Battalion, The Durham Light Infantry. These were all specially raised battalions for older men or those no longer fit for active service abroad. They were for home only service such as guarding bridges, ports, key installations, prisoner-of-war camps and training Home Guard units etc. On 17 December 1918 he died at the Military Hospital, Colchester, of influenza and broncho-pneumonia. His daughter Iris was born posthumously the following March in Burton-on-Trent, where Ethel had been brought up. In 1920 she remarried again and became Mrs Harry Savage.

George was awarded the 1914/15 Star and British War and Victory Medals.

Regimental Sergeant-Major Samuel Foster Gamble MC, 1st Battalion, The Leicestershire Regiment, No: 6419. Died 7 February 1919, aged 37.

Samuel was born in Hugglescote, Leicestershire, in 1881. His father James was a coal miner also born in Hugglescote and his mother Eliza was from Whitwick. Samuel worked as a colliery carter, but, on 5 July 1902 in Leicester, he enlisted for twelve years in The Leicestershire Regiment: active for three years and nine in reserve. He subsequently applied to change his service with the Colours to eight years and then again to twelve years. In 1903 he was promoted to Lance-Corporal, in 1904 to Corporal and in 1910 to Sergeant. His service up to the war was all spent at home with spells of duty at the Tower of London, Guernsey and Formoy, Ireland. In the 1911 census he is listed as a resident of Glen Parva Barracks.

On 28 September 1912 he married Ellen Bertha Randall of No. 53 Glengate, South Wigston, at St Thomas' Church. She was the daughter of Henry Randall a shoe worker. The couple made their home at No. 33 Irlam Street. They had a son, Reginald, who tragically died as a baby.

Following the outbreak of war he was posted overseas and on 9 September 1914 landed at St Navaire to join the Expeditionary Force. He was promoted to Colour-Sergeant in October 1914, Company Sergeant-Major in June 1916 and Regimental Sergeant-Major in December 1916. He was wounded in a gas attack on 19 December 1915, but after spells in hospital, was able to resume duties. He served four and a half years in France but became ill on 9 December 1918 with a cough and shortness of breath. He was transferred to England

on 9 January 1919 and admitted to the Military Hospital, High Barnet, where he
died on 7 February 1919 of heart disease and oedema.

Samuel was awarded the Military Cross, the 1914 Star and British War and
Victory Medals. Ellen remarried in late 1919 to Ernest H. Getliffe.

The grave of Regimental Sergeant-Major Samuel Foster Gamble MC in Wigston
Cemetery. (Tricia Berry)

Corporal George Marshall, 51st Battalion, The Northumberland Fusiliers, No: 94043. Died 31 March 1920, aged 19.

George was born in Chesterfield, Derbyshire, on 19 July 1900. He was the son of Herbert Marshall, a railway platelayer born in Claycross, Derbyshire, and his wife Mary Ann, born in Alnwick, Northumberland. In 1911 the family were living at No. 59 New Queen Street, Chesterfield, but subsequently moved to Albert Villa, Marstown Avenue, Glen Parva. George became a railway clerk, but towards the end of the war enlisted with The Northumberland Fusiliers. His choice of regiment was probably influenced by the fact that it was based in Alnwick, his mother's home town. He had been promoted Corporal, when, aged just 19, he died on 31 March 1920 at the Wharncliffe Military Hospital, Wadsley, Ecclesfield in Yorkshire, of military tuberculosis.

Unfortunately George's service papers do not appear to have survived, hence the brief account of his life.

Private Arthur Edward Cooper, The Leicestershire Regiment, No: 65371. Died 16 April 1920, aged 31.

Arthur was born in Humberstone, Leicester in 1889. He was the son of Frederick Cooper, a shoe laster, born in Leicester, and his wife Elizabeth, born in Herefordshire. He worked as a labourer, but on 2 April 1907 in Leicester enlisted for six years as a militia man (a civilian rather than professional role) with The Leicestershire Regiment. Two months later he transferred to become a full-time soldier with the 2nd Battalion. He served for several years in India, even appearing on the British 1911 census as a resident with fellow members of the 2nd Battalion at Fort Saint George, Madras. They were still in India when the war started and were summoned to France with all speed. Leaving on 5 August 1914 for the long journey, by land and sea, to France, they arrived on 11 October. Arthur suffered a severe gunshot wound to the side and was admitted to hospital in the field on 10 May 1915, and then transferred to England ten days later.

On 10 October 1915 he transferred to The Lincolnshire Regiment and returned to India with them on 25 November. He was appointed a Drummer in Calcutta on 24 March 1916, but by January 1918 was deprived of some first-class pay because of physical inefficiency. He retired but later re-joined The Leicestershire Regiment on 22 January 1919 for a period up until 31 March 1922.

On 7 June 1919 he married Beatrice Evans at St Stephen's Church, Leicester. Beatrice was a tailoress, the daughter of John Thomas Evans, a shoe hand. The couple made their home at No. 111 Lancaster Street, North Evington. Sadly, events overtook him and he died at the Military Hospital, Glen Parva Barracks, of pneumonia and cardiac failure on 16 April 1920.

He was awarded the 1914 Star and British War and Victory Medals.

Gertie Gitana, the music-hall entertainer who became known as the 'Tommies' favourite songbird. She raised several thousand pounds for war charities with concerts and the sale of signed postcards such as this one. She later married local impresario Don Ross and both are buried at Wigston Cemetery. (Tricia Berry)

Private Bertie Barratt, 12th Battalion, The Leicestershire Regiment,
No: 22720. Died 15 May 1920, aged 29.

Bertie was born in Wigston in 1891, the son of Amos Barratt, a railway examiner, and his wife Keziah, who were both born in Kilby. In 1911 the family lived in Victoria Street. He worked as an assistant carrier, but on 15 November 1915 joined The Leicestershire Regiment. On 5 June the following year he was discharged as unfit and issued with the Silver War Badge. This badge was issued to permanently sick or injured soldiers as a thank you for their service, and to show they had been in the forces and had been honourably discharged. Bertie did not serve overseas.

On 31 January 1918 at All Saints' Church he married Annie Harrison, the widow of Private Walter Harrison (*see* p. 95). At this time Bertie's occupation was motor driver. The couple went on to have a son named Bernard.

Bertie's health deteriorated and he received an army pension. He died on 15 May 1920 at the Ministry of Pensions Hospital, South Leicester of mitral disease and cardiac failure.

11

THE AFTERMATH
BY TRICIA BERRY

The Kaiser resigned on 9 November 1918 and two days later the Armistice was signed. It came into effect at 11 a.m. on 11 November 1918. The late Frank Noble, a South Wigston schoolboy at the time, has left us his memories of that momentous day (*see* chapter 2).

Life changed irrevocably due to the war, and the first few years afterwards saw much activity aimed at commemorating those who had died and improving the lives of those who had survived. Nationally, two important and far-reaching changes stand out. Firstly, the huge contribution women had made during the war, both at home and overseas, was recognised and without any further activity from the Suffragette movement most women aged 30 and above were given the vote. In 1928 this was amended to all women upon reaching the age of 21, in the same way as for men; secondly, the amalgamation of the five existing ex-service organisations into a new single stronger one, which was named the British Legion. It was officially launched on 1 July 1921, though its Unity Relief Fund had started acquiring the funds of the replaced organisations and other war relief charities, for some time before then. The Prince of Wales became the first patron, and Earl Haig the president. The creation of the British Legion was prompted by the shocking sight of some returning soldiers and sailors, both able bodied and disabled, begging in the streets, their plight partly due to the many strikes at this time, which led to the country being described as in a state of 'industrial collapse'.

In Wigston, as elsewhere, there was an acute housing shortage and in September 1919 the Council minutes recorded that it had obtained permission from the Local Government Board to borrow money for the purchase of land in Moat Street for the erection of workmen's houses. Similar building of these council houses was planned for Horsewell Lane and Aylestone Lane.

If landowners did not agree to sell, the Council would consider 'Compulsory Powers'. Two months later it is noted that they hoped to build: '65 houses with one living room, scullery and three bedrooms and 57 with parlour, living room, scullery and three bedrooms.' Government grants covered some of the building work but more was borrowed from the Liverpool Victoria Friendly Society. This loan was also for street works and to help with the cost of purchasing Newgate End Farm, which the Council wanted for use as a Scavenging Depot and for some of the proposed new houses.

When South Wigston was originally laid out, grassed recreational areas had been left at the end of each street, and these were now utilised for infill building.

Wigston Magna Urban District Council's offices were at No. 28 Station Road where many far-reaching decisions were made. This drawing shows the building in later years when in use as a Police Station. (Michael Clarke)

By July 1922 the minutes record that twenty-four houses had been completed but there was still a very pressing need. Councillor A.W. Holmes stated: 'People gave up their houses and stored their furniture when they were called up for war, and now on their return there were no houses to be had.' The situation was addressed, land was purchased, and from 1924 council homes were built in most of the streets to the north of Blaby Road.

The Government set up a Peace Committee to plan how the country would mark the end of the war, and Saturday 19 July 1919 was designated 'Peace Day', a day of national celebration.

The Leicester Daily Post of Monday 21 July 1919 displayed the front page headline: 'JOY DAY IN CITY, COUNTY AND CAPITAL'. Within its pages the activities in Wigston were described:

> The village was tastefully decorated, especially round the Bank. Soon after 10am a procession round the main streets was led by Wigston United Band followed by Boy Scouts and their band, members of the Council, discharged and demobilised soldiers and sailors, four decorated motor cars carrying wounded soldiers, decorated bicycles and fancy and comic decorated lorries and tableaux. Many of these were cleverly and artistically thought out, especially 'We kept the Home Fires Burning' (Mr Bailey) which won first prize. 'Peace' (Mr Crick) won second prize, 'Gipsy Encampment' (Mr Thacker) third prize and 'Hospital Ward' (Mr Jarvis) fourth prize. There were ten more decorated lorries, then the school children, and finally the Girl Guides. The procession went to The Orchards then returned, when the fancy dress prize winners were announced. They were 'Wanted, a House' (Masters Wood and Allen) and 'The Kaiser' (Mr A. Johnson). There was an address of welcome to returned warriors by Mr W.G. Forryan (Chairman of Wigston Magna Urban District Council) with further speeches by the Revd T.W. Wright, Revd Gari Phillips and Messrs Howe and Wignall. This was followed by sports on the recreation ground. The children then had tea at the Co-operative Hall and the National and Bell Street Schools.
>
> Later the soldiers and their wives and girlfriends had high tea at both Long Street Schools, 600 plus 700 sitting down. In the evening Mrs Cooper presented prizes at the Co-operative Hall, after which there was dancing and entertainment by Mr L. Burley's Troup of Pierrots from South Wigston.
>
> The arrangements were made by Wigston Benevolent Society of which Messrs W.H. Sharp and S.A. Ross were indefatigable honorary secretaries, assisted by Wigston Cycle Club (Mr J. Tebbutt) honorary secretary. Mr W. Measures was a most able marshall of the procession. Peels were rung on the Church bells all day.

'We Kept the Home Fires Burning' won first prize in the decorated drays competition at Wigston's Peace Day celebrations on 19 July 1919. From left to right: the Misses Lucas (Britannia), King (Peace), Herbert (Navy), Herbert and Possnett (Army), Randle (an old man), Copson (an old lady), children, Kitty Measures and N. Smith. Tom Mason is leading the horse. (Duncan Lucas)

The same paper reported on the celebrations which took place in South Wigston:

A procession headed by Wigston Temperance Silver Prize Band with Mr C. Moore, was followed by children from all the different churches, each group displaying its own banner, then the fancy dress, the decorated drays of which 'The Village Gossip' won first prize and 'Trial of the Kaiser' second prize, and finally numerous trucks and barrows of rag and bone merchants, houses wanted etc. Afterwards at a field lent by Mr Thornton of Crow Mills Farm the prizes were awarded and children's sports took place, followed by tea in their various schools.

Later the demobbed soldiers and sailors paraded to the sports ground, but because of rain the conclusion of their sports and the planned fireworks were held on the Monday instead. The soldiers and sailors and their partners, 800 in total, had a celebration tea at the Council schools where they were visited by councillors, before adjourning to the Clarence Assembly Rooms where prizes were presented by Councillors J.W. Black and A.W. Bruce. For the rest of the evening there was dancing and entertainment from Mr Bailey's Pierrots who had also given shows during the morning and afternoon … Mr T. Beeston and Mr J.T. Dodsley were honorary secretaries and Mr J.T. Stanton, chief marshall of the procession.

'Trial of the Kaiser' won second prize in the decorated drays competition at South Wigston's Peace Day celebrations on 19 July 1919. (Duncan Lucas)

Soldiers and sailors with their wives and girlfriends seated for their Peace Day Tea at the Girls' School, Bassett Street, South Wigston. (Peter Mastin)

A United Peace Service of the Anglican and Free Churches in Wigston was held at All Saints' Church on 6 July 1919. It was conducted by the Revd T.W. Wright, who was assisted by Revd J. Gari Phillips, minister of the Congregational Church in Long Street, and Mr A.H. Broughton, lay reader, of the Primitive Methodist Chapel in Cross Street. The three hymns chosen were: 'O God our help in ages past, Our hope for years to come', 'Father, let The Kingdom come – Let it come with living power', and 'God is working His purpose out as year succeeds to year'.

St Thomas' congregation decided to install a triple-faced clock in the tower, as a memorial to those who died in the war. It was dedicated on 14 June 1920 by the Lord Bishop of Peterborough. Leicester and the county were at this time in the diocese of Peterborough; the diocese of Leicester not being created until 1926.

All Saints' Church commemorated the Wigston men who lost their lives by installing a stained-glass memorial window, erecting below it a bronze tablet listing all 126 names. A shrine or roll of honour to their memory had already been created in the churchyard, which also included the names of the fallen. The artist of the window, Mr C.W. Whall, described his work as 'The Dragon, symbolising the late wicked crime against the human race … is subdued by St George bearing the Flag of the Lions of England and by St Michael who bears the Scales of Judgment. Above, the Sun of the Newer and Better Time rises …'

A Memorial and Dedication Service was held on Armistice Sunday, 14 November 1920. *The Leicester Daily Mercury* reported that: 'The parish church was filled to its utmost capacity … the congregation included a large number of relatives and friends of the fallen. The service … was conducted by the Vicar, Revd T.W. Wright, and music finely sung by the choir under the direction of Mr T. P. Barnes, Miss Violet Moore being at the organ … The plaque was unveiled by Lieutenant-Colonel Robert E. Martin CMG TD DL of Woodhouse Eaves.' (Robert Martin had a distinguished war record having been in command of the 1st/4th Territorial Battalion, The Leicestershire Regiment. He had bravely led his men when the Hohenzollen Redoubt was taken, but at huge cost, and was himself seriously wounded.) Both the window and the bronze tablet were then dedicated by the Lord Bishop of Peterborough who said: 'The best memorial to those who had gone was to carry on the war against sin and wrestle with the evils now so abundant … At the conclusion of the service the Last Post and Reveille were sounded and Miss Moore played Chopin's March Funebre as the congregation left the church. Before and after the service a half muffled peal of triple grandsires was rung on the bells.'

United Peace Service

of the Anglican and
Free Churches –

in the

Parish Church, Wigston Magna

Sunday July 6th, 1919, at 3 p.m.

Conducted by

Rev. T. W. Wright, M.A.

Assisted by

Rev. J. Gari Phillips, B.A.

and

Mr. A. H. Broughton.

Collection for the Wigston Peace Memorial Fund.

DEEMING BROS. PRINTERS

Order of service for the United Peace Service held at All Saints' Church, 6 July 1919. (Tricia Berry)

All Saints' Church, Wigston Magna

SUNDAY NOVEMBER 14th, 1920,

AT 11 A.M.,

The Holy Eucharist will be offered as

The Memorial Service

On behalf of the Wigston Men and Lads who gave their lives in the Great War 1914—1918.

— THE —

Lord Bishop of Peterborough

WILL BE PRESENT AT THE SERVICE AND PREACH
AND WILL AFTERWARDS

Dedicate the Memorial Window and Bronze Tablet

WHICH WILL BE UNVEILED BY

Lt. Col. R. E. MARTIN, C.M.G., T.D., D.L.

Places in the body of the Church will be reserved UNTIL 10-45 A.M., AND NOT LATER, for Relatives and Friends of the Men who gave their lives. It is hoped that as many as possible of those who wish to receive Communion on this day will do so at one of the early services (7 a.m. or 8 a.m.) so as not to unduly lengthen the eleven o'clock service. Floral tributes if brought by friends should be handed to Sidesmen on duty in the Church who will place them in the Chancel or on the War Shrine.

The Collection at the Offertory, after necessary expenses, will be given to Red Cross Relief Work.

The artist, Mr. C. W. Whall, gives the following description of the Memorial Window : "The leading idea of the window is the passing of the reign of violence and the coming of the reign of law and of love. The Dragon, symbolizing the late wicked crime against the human race with destruction and conflagration in his train, is subdued by S. George bearing the Flag of the Lions of England and by S. Michael who bears the Scales of Judgment. Above, the Sun of the Newer and Better Time rises surrounded by Seraphim and Cherubim the agents of the Heavenly Love and Heavenly Wisdom."

Below the Window a Bronze has upon it the names of the Wigston men who gave their lives.

Order of service for the Unveiling and Dedication of the Memorial Window and Bronze Tablet at All Saints' Church on 14 November 1920. (Wigston Parish Magazine)

Roll of Honour that records 126 names in All Saints' Churchyard. (Tricia Berry)

DE 5310

SOUTH WIGSTON AND GLEN PARVA
WAR MEMORIAL

·:·

Unveiling & Dedication

BY

Major General Sir E. M. Woodward

K.C.M.G., C.B.,

Colonel of the Leicestershire Regiment,

AND

The Venerable F. B. Macnutt, M.A.

Archdeacon of Leicester.

·:·

SUNDAY, NOVEMBER 11th, 1923,

AT 2.30 P.M.

Order of service for the Unveiling and Dedication of the War Memorial at South Wigston on 11 November 1923. (Record Office for Leicestershire, Leicester and Rutland)

The South Wigston Benevolent Committee wished to erect a war
memorial to the local fallen. On 6 July 1920, Wigston Magna Urban District
Council approved the site chosen for The South Wigston and Glen Parva War
Memorial, which was to be erected on land next to St Thomas' Church.
A ceremony of Unveiling and Dedication took place on Armistice Sunday,
11 November 1923. Everyone taking part assembled at the Council Schools.
The ex-servicemen, wearing their medals and decorations, then marched
to the Depot Square at the Barracks led by the band of the 1st Battalion,
The Leicestershire Regiment, which had travelled from Aldershot especially
for the occasion. Other guests formed another procession led by Mr Charles
Moore with his Wigston Temperance Silver Prize Band. They joined
relatives of the fallen soldiers for a service led by The Venerable Frederick
Brodie Macnutt MA, Archdeacon of Leicester and Vicar of St Martin's church,
Leicester, who, as a padre, was wearing his own medals.
  On the platform were:

Major-General Sir E.M. Woodward KCMG CB, Colonel of
The Leicestershire Regiment
Major F. Latham DSO OC, the Depot, Glen Parva
Major W.G. Stanhope Rolleston DL JP (who lived in Saffron Road and was
the brother of the late Sir John Rolleston of Glen Parva Grange)
The Venerable F.B. Macnutt MA, Archdeacon of Leicester
The Revd C.W. Weston, Vicar of St Thomas' Church, South Wigston,
and Officiating Chaplain to the Forces
The Revd W.S. Hinchcliffe and The Revd W.J. Manistre
Councillor A.S. Payne (Wigston Magna Urban District Council)

Other notable guests were: Mr A. Turner, High Sherriff, Lieutenant-Colonel
R.E. Martin, Colonel H. Gordon, Colonel E.L. Challoner, Colonel A.W.S.
Brock, Colonel C.F. Oliver and Revd J.T. Coward.
  Following the service there was a procession to the War Memorial
in the following order: Guard of Honour, Officials and Committee,
Guests, Wigston Temperance Silver Prize Band, Choirs, 1st Battalion,
The Leicestershire Regiment Band, ex-servicemen, British Legion,
Independent Order of Good Templars, Independent Order of Foresters,
Independent Order of Odd-fellows, Independent Order of Rechabites,
Sportsmen, Ideal Benefit Society, three divisions of the St John's Ambulance
Brigade and schoolchildren.
  The Leicester Daily Mercury of 12 November 1923 reported:

At the Memorial, in the presence of 6,000 people ... there was a further short service and a speech by Major Rolleston. Major-General Woodward then said ... England owed a never ending debt of love to her soldiers ... we had been led away by phrases ... told that the war was fought to make 'a land fit for heroes to live in' ... to make 'England Safe for Democracy' ... 'the war to end all wars', but the war was fought because the British race in every quarter of the globe was determined to stand up for right and protect the weak from the oppression of the strong ... He then unveiled the Memorial.

The Archdeacon followed with ... The world today, five years after the Armistice was not worthy of the great sacrifice by the men they were there to honour this afternoon ... unless we make ourselves more worthy, we shall deserve what we have been told by the wisest men will come upon us ... There followed The Last Post ... Reveille (the shrill notes of the bugles being emphasised by the roar of maroons) ... one minute's silence, prayers, and the National Anthem ... after which there was the laying of floral tributes on the Memorial.

There are 104 men from the Great War commemorated on the South Wigston and Glen Parva War Memorial. The number of different regiments they belonged to suggests some might not be locals, but men from other areas who died while patients at the Barracks Hospital. One notable name is that of Lieutenant-Colonel John Mosse, the Commandant at the Barracks. He had collapsed in the orderly room and died on 17 June 1916, aged only 56.

Huge crowds attended the Unveiling and Dedication of the Memorial at South Wigston. (Record Office for Leicestershire, Leicester and Rutland)

Postcard photograph of members of the Wigston Benevolent Society who raised money to help local people both at home and abroad. (Tricia Berry)

Wigston had a Benevolent Society as well as South Wigston. It was established in 1916, the initial object being to: 'help village folk in need through illness and other causes'. The Vicar was made Chairman, Mr Bert Hassall the Treasurer, and Mr Measures, of Leicester Road, the Honorary Secretary. They raised funds through subscriptions, donations, concerts and band parades etc. The two branches, Wigston and South Wigston, were flexible and also offered assistance wherever it was needed, such as sending parcels to local men who were prisoners of war, assisting with the Victory Day parades and, as mentioned previously, helping to promote the idea of a war memorial for South Wigston and Glen Parva.

War memorials were also established by many, if not all, of the local independent churches and chapels as a tribute to former members of their own congregations. The Council and some of the larger businesses did the same. One such was W. Dunmore & Son Ltd., biscuit manufacturers, of Canal Street, which built an open-air swimming pool for the village, next to the canal and recreation ground at the end of Park Road, as a tribute to employees lost in the war. A tablet recording their names stood at the entrance. This was hugely popular with local youngsters in the hot summers of the 1920s and early 1930s, but following a nationwide typhoid scare, fell into disuse and was eventually demolished.

At a special meeting of Wigston Magna Urban District Council, held on 25 November 1918, with Mr W.G. Forryan in the Chair, the following statement was read out: 'Mr A.E. Hill states that there is a general feeling in the

District that arrangements should be made to commemorate the signing of the Peace and suggests that the committees of the existing war charities should be invited to combine with the Council in carrying this into effect.' It was moved by Mr Hill and seconded by Mr F. Thorpe and carried unanimously: 'That the Council are willing to take the lead in any steps that may be agreed upon for celebrating the signing of the Peace and for the provision of a combined Peace Memorial Park.'

In December it was noted that: 'The Carnegie Trust be approached by the Clerk for a grant towards the provision in each part of the Districts of an Institute with a free Library attached.' By early January 1919: 'Schemes for suitable Peace Commemoration Memorials in both sections of the District are in course of preparation and the committee arranging them for South Wigston have asked the Council for approval to purchase Benjamin Toone's property at the corner of Blaby Road and Canal Street to convert to an Institute.'

On 20 March 1919, at another Special Meeting, a deputation from the Peace Memorial Committee reported on their progress to the Council. The deputation consisted of Mr A.H. Broughton (of A.H. Broughton & Co., hosiery manufacturers, Bull Head Street), Mr J.W. Black CC (of J.W. Black & Co., boot and shoe manufacturers, Saffron Road), Mr A.R. Deeming (of Deeming Brothers, printers of South Wigston), Mr G. Hewitt, Mr C.E. Hurst (Director of Cook & Hurst Ltd., hosiery and underwear manufacturers, of No. 8 Long Street) and Mr Edward Lee (Managing Director of Two Steeples Ltd., Leicester Road). A.H. Broughton

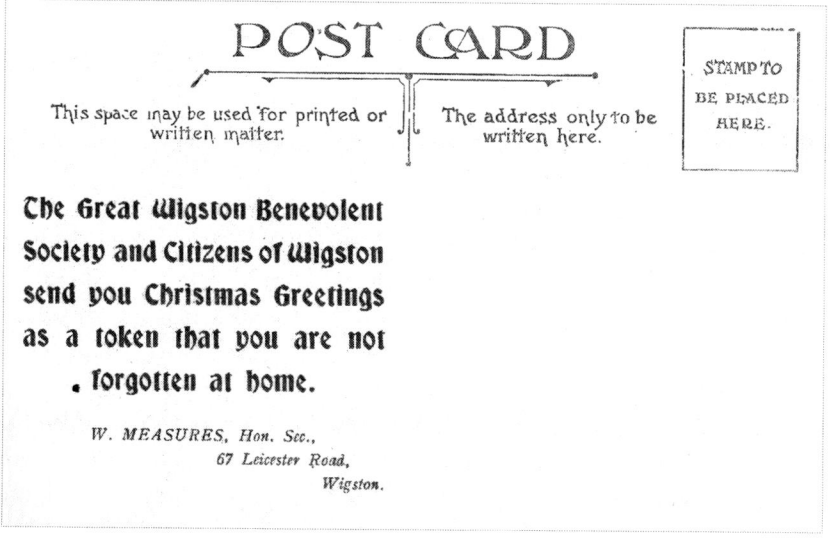

Reverse of the postcard with a Christmas message to accompany parcels for troops serving overseas.

reported that: 'At a public meeting to consider the park it was decided to accept Mr A.E. Hill's offer to sell a portion of Gaol Close with a view to laying it out as a Peace Park with Tennis Courts and Bowling Green, and also an Institute (the site of which Mr Hill is willing to give), at an estimated cost of £4,000.'

The conditions of Mr Hill's offer were:

1. A laurel hedge and shrubbery be planted within 21 feet of the present cottage boundary so as to secure privacy for the park and cottages, but no large trees to overshadow.
2. That a bungalow type pavilion be built in the park, with a veranda facing the green, that could serve as a reading room, Institute Club House and Tea Room and be used free by disabled soldiers and sailors. The grounds to be kept in order by two disabled men. Children under 16 not allowed in the grounds unless accompanied by an adult. A Sanitary Block for the public and park to be sited near the road. Upkeep of the whole to be born by the council and the Sanitary Block erected at the cost of the Council.

Gaol (or Jail) Close was a small field of approximately 2.5 acres before it became the Peace Memorial Park. It was once part of the Wigston Hall estate, which was on the opposite side of the road, and was used as a paddock. The name is believed to originate from the time of the Civil War, when, due to a shortage of food, prisoners were moved there from Leicester Prisons.

Albert Edward Hill had purchased Gaol Close on 4 October 1918 from the Clarke family who had owned it for many years. He had been much involved in public life throughout the war and was Chairman of the Council in 1916/17. It seems highly likely he bought the close, just a month before the Armistice was signed, realising the war must end soon, and with the park idea in mind.

When the Council met on 6 May 1919 it was agreed by nine votes in favour and six against that the offer presented on 20 March should be accepted. The six who voted against were all the South Wigston councillors, including Mr Black who had previously been in support. It seems likely that South Wigston residents had decided, understandably, that the park plan in Wigston was too far away for them to be able to use.

On 12 May 1919 Mr Black reported that: 'The South Wigston War Memorial Committee are preparing a scheme for laying out a plot of land as a public garden and they desire the boundary fence to be taken up to the kerb in each of the three streets to which the land fronts so as to include the site of the causeways.' Nothing more is mentioned about this scheme or the plans for the two Institutes and Libraries. It appears that the Carnegie Trust was unwilling to make a grant towards the Institute and Library of either district.

On 2 March 1920, Mr Broughton reported to the Council that: 'The Great Wigston Peace Memorial Committee are unable to carry out their scheme in its entirety but they are prepared to offer to the Council the Park laid out as approved, but without the Institute owing to the cost of building.' The Council agreed to accept the revised offer.

The Peace Memorial Park Committee now had to undertake some serious fundraising. The Wigston Magna Prisoner of War Fund, which was established to raise money for parcels to be sent to the thirty-five Wigston men in captivity, had spare funds following the Armistice, and its committee agreed that this, and the proceeds of a planned bazaar, should be given to the Park fund. Other war charities who suddenly found themselves with superfluous funds probably did the same. Schoolchildren helped raise money by encouraging everyone to donate for a mile of pennies, which was laid out round the village.

When sufficient money was raised to buy the land, three leading members of the Park Committee, Alonzo Harry Broughton, Charles Edwin Hurst and John Ernest Rawson (Company Secretary at Two Steeples Ltd., hosiery manufacturers, Leicester Road), 'acting in accordance with the wishes of the subscribers to the fund and other inhabitants of Old Wigston', became the purchasers and paid £741 5s 0d to Albert Edward Hill, the vendor, for Gaol Close. It was agreed the land would not be conveyed at this time,

An early view of the Peace Memorial Park showing seating round the base of some very mature trees. (Duncan Lucas)

but that the park would be set out as planned by the Park Committee, and then conveyed jointly by all four gentlemen to the Council which had agreed to accept it and maintain it in the future.

Creation of the new park then commenced. Alexander Pawley of Junction Road, a landscape gardener, was employed by the Park Committee to lead the work. Ex-servicemen were invited to plant some of the trees and shrubs. In November the Committee offered to set back the fence of the proposed park in Long Street in order to widen the road, providing the Council agreed to flag the causeway, an area of about 50 square yards. By Saturday 9 April 1921 all was sufficiently ready for the conveyance to be signed and the park officially opened.

On the Monday *The Leicester Mercury* reported:

Efforts are now being made to provide a cenotaph for the Memorial Park at Old Wigston which was formerly opened on Saturday. Dr Barnley presided and said they should try to live up to the Memorial and make Wigston an ideal village, with pretty gardens and window boxes, a place for heroes to live in. However, he thought the park was not complete without a memorial and suggested that a cenotaph be erected with the names of everyone who gave their lives in the Great War upon it ... so that passers-by might know what the park was for. Several other speakers endorsed the idea ... it being pointed out that Oadby, Great Glen and Evington had memorials in course of erection ... Mr A.H. Broughton said out of a population of 9,000 people, 1,850 had joined the colours, of whom 200 were killed and 500 maimed or wounded, a record he said was second to none in any town or village in England ... Mr C.E. Hurst said people had been very generous, £1,994 5s 6d had been subscribed but the expenses had been £2241 13s 6d leaving an adverse balance of £247 8s 0d which he hoped would be immediately cleared off ... The late Mr Fielding Johnson had kindly given the railings which were cleaned and erected free of cost by Mr Matthews, while Herbert Simpson undertook all the legal work, free of cost, even to paying out of pocket expense ... Mr J.W. Black had made a generous offer to assist in wiping out the deficit.

Thomas Fielding Johnson lived at Brookfield, London Road, Leicester, and owned a substantial yarn-spinning business in the town. It was he who bought the old Lunatic Asylum buildings in Victoria Road (later University Road) Leicester, which had served as 5th Northern General Hospital during the Great War. When the war ended he bought the whole property including about 30 acres of land and gave it to the City for a university

Members of the newly formed Wigston Bowling Club. It is believed the two people in
the middle row (seated on chairs) are, third from left, A.E. Crane and, fourth from left,
A.H. Broughton. (Arthur Harrison)

and also sites for Wyggeston Boys' and Girls' Schools. He died in March 1921,
aged 93, so the gift of these railings was probably his last act of generosity.

On 19 April 1921 the Council reported the appointing of a Park Standing
Committee, which consisted of: 'Messrs A.H. Broughton, A.E. Crane,
A.R. Deeming, J.H. Holmes, H.A. Snowden, F. Thorpe and T.W. Wright
(the Vicar).' This committee advertised for a caretaker and received six
applications but chose their landscape gardener, Alexander Pawley, who
remained in post for many years. By 3 May, Mr Crane had: 'offered to fix
seats round some of the trees ... apparatus for lawn tennis and bowls was
to be purchased ... and the Bye Laws would be submitted for adoption by
the Council very soon.' On 26 May: 'Since the Park opened for games it has
been well patronised.' By July: 'The following had offered to supply seats,
A.H. Broughton, Messrs Holmes & Son, Employees of the Co-operative
Society, W.E. Broughton and W.E. Huckerby (of Leeds).'

It is clear that raising the money for the park project was an uphill struggle,
with original plans having to be much curtailed. The park did not have a
pavilion until the Bowling Club had one built in 1928. It was eventually sold
to the council in 1939. The cenotaph idea never materialised, though happily in
recent times this has been remedied by the lovely, peaceful, remembrance corner
with wreaths and plaques listing the names of those lost in both world wars.

The Bowling Club was founded in 1921 and first began to play in the park in 1922. Officers elected were:

President –	Mr A.H. Broughton, who served from 1922–36
Vice Presidents –	Messrs F. Boulter, G. Boulter, B. Broughton, E. Broughton, E. Bailey, A.E. Crane, A.R. Deeming, B. Hackett, H. Holmes, C.E. Hurst, A.G. Shipp and Revd J.G. Phillips, and Revd T.W. Wright
Treasurer –	Mr A. Hurst
Secretary –	Mr J. Sutherland
Captain –	Mr T. Norman
Vice-Captain –	Mr F. Simpson

BIBLIOGRAPHY

BOOKS

Armitage, F.P., *Leicester 1914–1918: the Wartime Story of a Midland Town* (Leicester, 1933)
Beazley, Ben, *Four Years Remembered: Leicester During the Great War* (Derby, 1999)
Broughton, Janice, *A Golden Age 1889–1914* (Wigston, 2011)
Greening, E.O., *A Democratic Co-Partnership* (Leicester, 1921)
Kind, Alan Orson, MBE, *Memories of One Family* (2012)
Noble, Frank, *History of South Wigston* (Wigston, 1979)
Rawson, Andrew, *British Army Handbook 1914–1918* (Stroud, 2006)
Richardson, Matthew, *The Tigers: 6th, 7th, 8th, 9th (Service) Battalions of The Leicestershire Regiment* (Barnsley, 2000)
Seaton, Derek, *A Tiger and A Fusilier: Leicester's VC Heroes* (Botcheston, 2001)
_____, *This Gallant Steelback: William Ewart Boulter VC* (Leicester, 2010)
Ward, Pamela, *Wigston at War* (South Wigston, 2004)

NEWSPAPERS

Illustrated Leicester Chronicle
Leicester Advertiser
The Leicester Chronicle and Leicestershire Mercury
The Leicester Daily Mercury
The Leicester Daily Post
The Leicester Mail

OTHER SOURCES

Various church records, the minutes of the Wigston Urban District Council and Burial Registers and other relevant documents held by the Record Office for Leicestershire, Leicester and Rutland
All Saints' church parish and District Free Churchman magazines
Greater Wigston Historical Society transactions 49, 73 and 74
First World War military service papers

Also from The History Press

GREAT WAR BRITAIN

Great War Britain is a unique new local series to mark the centenary of the Great War. In partnership with archives and museums across Great Britain, the series provides an evocative portrayal of life during this 'war to end all wars'. In a scrapbook style, and beautifully illustrated, it includes features such as personal memoirs, letters home, diary extracts, newspaper reports, photographs, postcards and other local First World War ephemera.

GREAT WAR BRITAIN

BRADFORD
Remembering 1914–18

Dr KATHRYN HUGHES
IN ASSOCIATION WITH BRADFORD LIBRARIES
AND WEST YORKSHIRE ARCHIVES SERVICE

GREAT WAR BRITAIN

OXFORDSHIRE
Remembering 1914–18

JANE COTTER
IN ASSOCIATION WITH THE
SOLDIERS OF OXFORDSHIRE MUSEUM

Find these titles and more at
www.thehistorypress.co.uk

The History Press

Also from The History Press

LUCY ADLINGTON

GREAT
WAR
FASHION

TALES FROM
THE HISTORY WARDROBE

Find this title and more at
www.thehistorypress.co.uk

Also from The History Press

BLOODY BRITISH HISTORY

Britain has centuries of incredible history to draw on – everything from Boudica and the Black Death to the Blitz. This local series, harking back to the extraordinary pulp magazines of days gone by, contains only the darkest and most dreadful events in your area's history. So embrace the nastier side of British history with these tales of riots and executions, battles and sieges, murders and regicides, witches and ghosts, death, devilry and destruction!

Find these titles and more at
www.thehistorypress.co.uk

Also from The History Press

WHEN DISASTER STRIKES

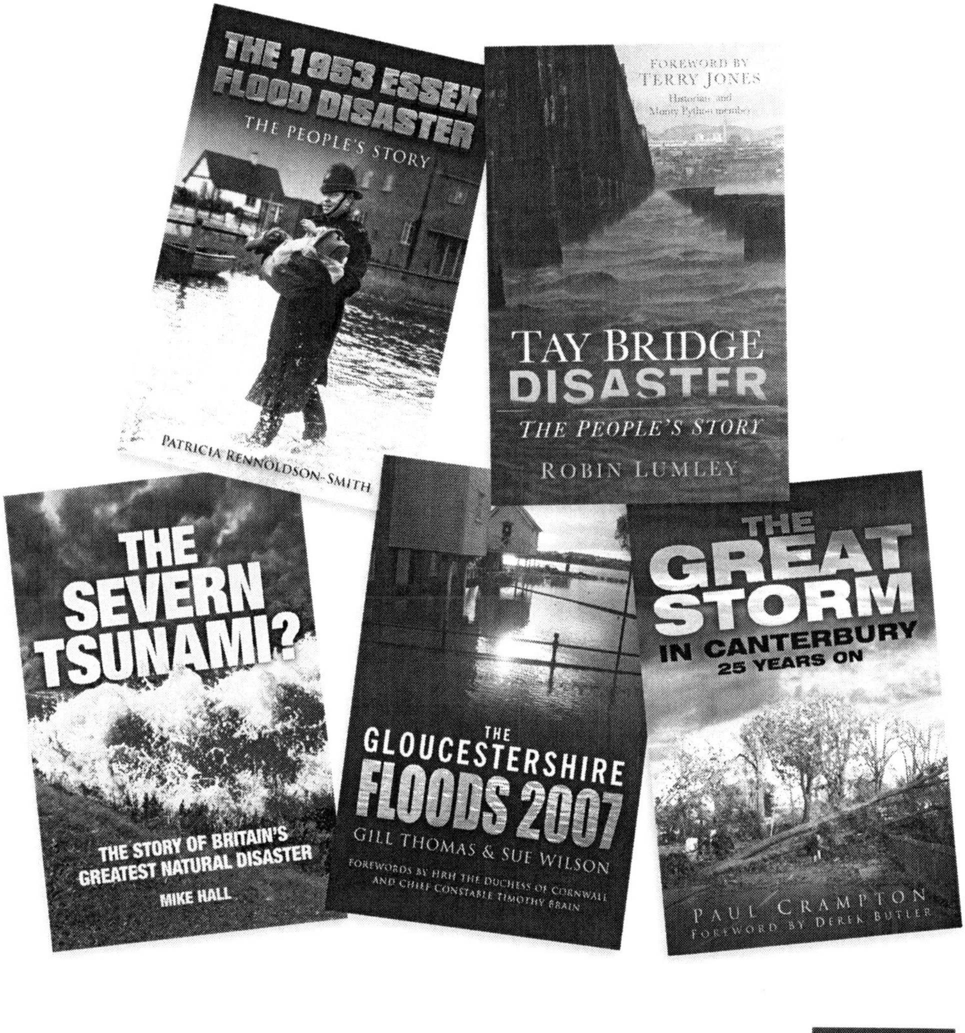

THE 1953 ESSEX FLOOD DISASTER
THE PEOPLE'S STORY
PATRICIA RENNOLDSON-SMITH

FOREWORD BY TERRY JONES
Historian and Monty Python member
TAY BRIDGE DISASTER
THE PEOPLE'S STORY
ROBIN LUMLEY

THE SEVERN TSUNAMI?
THE STORY OF BRITAIN'S GREATEST NATURAL DISASTER
MIKE HALL

THE GLOUCESTERSHIRE FLOODS 2007
GILL THOMAS & SUE WILSON
FOREWORDS BY HRH THE DUCHESS OF CORNWALL AND CHIEF CONSTABLE TIMOTHY BRAIN

THE GREAT STORM IN CANTERBURY 25 YEARS ON
PAUL CRAMPTON
FOREWORD BY DEREK BUTLER

Find these titles and more at
www.thehistorypress.co.uk

The History Press

Lightning Source UK Ltd.
Milton Keynes UK
UKOW04f1354090614

233094UK00001B/18/P